KARADSHEH'S
SPICE BAZAAR

COOKBOOK

*An adventure in fine cuisine
from the Middle East, Greece
and around the world*

Mary Ajalat Karadsheh

Published by Karadsheh's Spice Bazaar, Inc.®

FIRST EDITION, July 1994
SECOND EDITION
First Printing, December 2000
Second Printing, June 2001
Third Printing, October 2002
Fourth Printing, October 2003
Fifth Printing, September 2005
Sixth Printing, August 2007

Copyright © 1994, 2000 by Karadsheh's Spice Bazaar, Inc.®
1-800-30-SPICE
(1-800-307-7423)
www.spicebazaar.com
e-mail: paymon@spicebazaar.com

Printed in the United States of America

ISBN 0-9706251-0-3

DEDICATION

To my beloved husband, Shafik.
We shared forty years of joy and hard work
and five beautiful children.
His encouragement and patience
allowed me to develop
my recipes and perfect my blends.
He left me for a better place one year ago.
I miss him dearly.

MY SECOND EDITION

I am very excited to present this second edition of the *SPICE BAZAAR COOKBOOK*, which introduces many new recipes, improvements on earlier favorites and three new sections.

The "Desserts" section includes my recipes for Baklava and Rice Pudding, the two most popular desserts in the Middle Eastern Bakery & Deli, along with many other Greek and Arabic favorites. The "Breads" section includes our family's recipe for Talamee (Syrian Bread), which will bring back happy memories to many of their mothers baking this delicious, simple bread at home. The aroma of baked Tsoureki (Greek Easter Bread) will remind many of Easter at Yiayia and Papou's house. As a member of the Eastern Orthodox Christian Church, I have had many people ask that I share my recipe for the Holy Bread that is used during our Liturgies. I also have included my recipe for Memorial Wheat, which is offered when a loved one passes away. My third new section, "Tips, Tricks and Special Recipes", includes a glossary of ingredients, substitution information, kitchen shortcuts, instructions on handling filo dough and other trade secrets.

ACKNOWLEDGEMENTS

This second edition couldn't have been completed without the help and support of many special people. My daughters and their husbands, Angela Karadsheh Kreta and Stephen Kreta, Mona Karadsheh Soot and Fr. Stephen Soot, Deena Karadsheh, and Randa Karadsheh Anderson and Keith Anderson, and my son John's future bride, Natascha Ovando, have endured hours of phone calls, e-mails and endless proofreading sessions. Their creativity and insight have added immeasurably to this exciting second edition. I especially want to thank my son, John, who shouldered the burden of managing the Middle Eastern Bakery & Deli, while I was so deeply immersed in this project. His quick smile and words of support were always there when I needed them the most.

My kitchen staff at the Middle Eastern Bakery and Deli, under the direction of Mariana Ramirez, has been patient and helpful with the months of recipe testing. Our Deli grocery manager, Majdi Almasri, has been an important and continuing resource for information on Arabic ingredients and recipes. My assistant, Chef Bill Seese, has been invaluable in analyzing recipes and helping me to update my website and getting it to run smoothly. Todd Templeton has come to my aid numerous times with computer help and Internet advice. I also want to thank Jantzen Moser for formatting my book, and Drew Templeton, Page DeMello and many other good friends for taking the time to proofread and test the recipes.

TABLE OF CONTENTS

A BIT OF HISTORY

My interest in cooking goes back to the days of standing by my mother's side as she lovingly prepared meals for our family. When she first came to this country from Jordan in the 1930's, she found the variety of foods available very exciting. As her new American friends introduced her to many dishes, she would go home to her kitchen and work to duplicate the flavors. My mother's example sparked in me a desire to create recipes using many unusual spices.

In 1978, my husband, Shafik, and I bought the Middle Eastern Bakery and Deli in Phoenix, Arizona. Our goal was to change a simple Arabic bread bakery into a busy, vibrant food emporium. As I expanded the deli menu with many new dishes, I was faced with the challenge of how to maintain consistency of flavors. I found that by developing a unique spice blend for each recipe, there was little chance for error in the preparation of the dishes. As our deli's reputation for flavorful and unique foods grew, the demand for my recipes and spices also grew. By bottling my spice blends, I was able to share my trade secrets with my customers. Thus, *SPICE BAZAAR* was born.

Five years ago our son, John, joined the family business, bringing his own creative flare to our deli and to *SPICE BAZAAR*. After my husband, Shafik, passed away in 1999, John took over management of the Deli, freeing my time to develop *SPICE BAZAAR* further. Writing this expanded edition of the "*SPICE BAZAAR COOKBOOK*" has been a very exciting priority for me. It is our hope that through *SPICE BAZAAR* you will embark on an adventure of new tastes and textures to awaken your palate and enliven your table.

"SAHTEIN"

صحتين

TO YOUR HEALTH!!!

HEALTHY EATING
WITH REAL SATISFACTION
AND PLEASURE

Because of my interest in nutrition, I have developed my recipes using a reduced amount of fat and salt wherever possible. Some of the blends include salt in a moderate amount. If salt is not a health concern, you may want to add more to taste. Fat in the recipes can be reduced even further with some simple adjustments.

- Use boneless, skinless breasts in place of whole chicken.
- Use extra-lean beef and lamb.
- Substitute all or part ground turkey for the beef and lamb.
- Eliminate oil for sautéing by using a non-stick pan and a non-stick spray.
- Use nonfat or lowfat yogurt, sour cream and mayonnaise, in place of the full fat versions.

New health concepts tend to favor the moderate use of butter over margarine as the trans fats in margarine are considered more harmful than the saturated fat in butter. For this reason, I use butter and olive oil instead of margarine in my recipes. However, margarine may be used if preferred.

I have marked vegan/Lenten ✤ and vegetarian ◆ recipes so that those who are looking for these healthful dishes can locate them easily. Also marked with these symbols are recipes which can be adapted to vegan/Lenten or vegetarian. This is easily accomplished by substituting oil for butter, by using vegetable broth in place of chicken broth, or by using fish in place of meat or chicken. The index has a complete "Vegetarian and Vegan/Lenten" section for quick reference.

"YASOU"

Ψασου!

TO YOUR HEALTH!!!

18 BLENDS TO ENHANCE YOUR TABLE

See **INDEX BY SPICE BLEND** (page 168) for recipes using each blend.

ATHENIAN GARDEN SPICE
Originally developed as a seasoning for vegetable soup, this blend livens any vegetable recipe and adds delightful flavor to baked fish and chicken.

Ingredients: Salt, Onion, Herbs and Spices (Allspice, Basil, Cinnamon, Cloves, Coriander, Fennel, Savory, Sumac, Thyme, White and Black Pepper and others), Garlic, Cornstarch, Citric, Sugar, Calcium Phosphate (prevents caking).

DAMASCUS KIBBIE SPICE
With this perfectly balanced spice, the classic dish, "Kibbie", can be prepared easily every time. Use it to prepare other dishes including Samboosiks (Meat-filled Filo Rolls) and Lamb Ouzi (Lamb and Rice Platter).

Ingredients: Salt, Spices (Allspice, Cinnamon, Cloves, Coriander, Black Pepper and others).

EGYPTIAN LENTIL SOUP SPICE
Prepare hearty and satisfying lentil soup for your family. You will find the addition of *EGYPTIAN LENTIL SOUP SPICE* also improves the flavor of meats, vegetables, eggs and dressings.

Ingredients: Salt, Onion, Spices (Allspice, Cardamom, Cloves, Coriander, Cumin, Nutmeg, White Pepper and others), Garlic, Citric.

ETHIOPIAN HOT SPICE*
Add zip to your meals with this authentic Ethiopian hot and spicy blend. Add some to your favorite dip and sauce recipes. Keep it on your table to add zest to any dish you serve. For a quick and easy one-dish meal, try "Ethiopian Chicken Stew". You control the heat by the amount of spice you add.

Ingredients: Spices (Black and Brown Caraway, Cinnamon, Coriander, Cumin, Curry, Fenugreek, Black Pepper, Turmeric and others), Chile, Cayenne.

GARAM MASALA INDIAN BLEND*
SPICE BAZAAR'S version of this classic Indian blend is used in New Delhi Eggplant Stew and in soups, sauces and on marinated meats, chicken and fish.

Ingredients: Spices (Cardamom, Cinnamon, Cloves, Coriander, Cumin, Black Pepper and others).

GREEK SALAD DRESSING BLEND
This blend bursts with flavor and perks up even the simplest dish. Easily whip up dressing for Greek Salad or your favorite greens. Also use it to prepare delicious Greek Marinade and Greek Home-baked Potatoes.

Ingredients: Salt, Garlic, Herbs and Spices (Basil, Greek Oregano, Black Pepper and others), Onion, Lemon Juice Powder, Citric, Gum Tragacanth (emulsifier), Calcium Phosphate (prevents caking).

* Salt Free

HELLENIC HERB BLEND*
Greek cooking has always been known for its wonderful use of herbs. Spanakopitas, Keftedes and other traditional Greek dishes can now be prepared in your home with complete success using this balanced combination of herbs and spices.

Ingredients: Onion, Garlic, Herbs and Spices (Basil, Dill, Greek Oregano, Parsley, Black Pepper and others).

HERBES DE FRANCE*
This aromatic blend of herbs enhances the flavor of cheese, vegetables and fish. It is wonderful in sauces and cream cheese dips. Prepare piquant Herbed French Vinaigrette and French Artichoke Dip with HERBES DE FRANCE.

Ingredients: Herbs (Basil, Fennel, French Lavender, Savory, Thyme and others).

JERICHO FALAFEL SPICE
This blend simplifies the preparation of Falafel so that you are assured of success every time. Recipes in this book use JERICHO FALAFEL SPICE to enliven the flavor of soups, chicken and fish.

Ingredients: Spices (Coriander, Cumin, White Pepper and others), Salt, Garlic, Cayenne.

JERUSALEM HUMMUS SPICE
Use this blend with chick peas and sesame tahini paste to prepare the most popular dip in the Middle East. Perfect Hummus takes less than five minutes made the SPICE BAZAAR way. Also use this blend to prepare Avgolemono Sauce, Meatless Malfoof (Cabbage Rolls) and other exciting recipes.

Ingredients: Garlic, Salt, Lemon Juice Powder, Citric, Calcium Phosphate (prevents caking).

JORDANIAN ROAST LAMB SPICE
Prepare succulent Roast Leg of Lamb, Jordanian Tajin (Oven-baked Lamb Stew) and Sheikh El Mahshi (Stuffed Eggplant Boats), with this exotic blend. It also works wonders with ordinary roast beef.

Ingredients: Spices (Allspice, Cardamom, Cloves, Coriander, Nutmeg, Black Pepper and others), Salt, Garlic, Onion, Citric.

LEBANESE KIFTA SPICE
Originally created for seasoning kabobs, this has become one of our most popular and versatile blends. It adds unique flavor to chicken, stews, potatoes, eggs and sauces.

Ingredients: Salt, Spices (Cinnamon, Black Pepper, Sumac and others), Garlic, Cornstarch, Citric, Calcium Phosphate (prevents caking).

* Salt Free

MIDDLE EASTERN BLEND*
This blend, which is called *Bharat* (Mixed Spices) in Arabic, enhances the flavor of many traditional Arabic foods. It is perfect for all types of stews, baked chicken and meat dishes. Use it to prepare outstanding Shish-kabob.

Ingredients: Spices (Allspice, Cardamom, Cinnamon, Cloves, Coriander, Cumin, Nutmeg, Black Pepper and others).

MOROCCAN BLEND
Create traditional Moroccan Couscous and Moroccan Baked Chicken with this blend of true North African flavors. **MOROCCAN BLEND** complements the flavor of fish, poultry and vegetables.

Ingredients: Salt, Spices (Cinnamon, Cloves, Curry, Ginger, Spanish Saffron, Turmeric and others).

RANDA'S SPICE
This blend was created by the author to simplify a recipe for fried chicken that her 10 year old daughter, Randa, loved to prepare. It is used in many dishes in combination with other **SPICE BAZAAR BLENDS** to balance and round out the recipe flavors. Keep it on your table in place of the salt shaker.

Ingredients: Salt, Onion, Black Pepper, Hungarian Paprika, Garlic, Citric, Sugar, Calcium Phosphate (prevents caking).

SESAME TAHINI SAUCE AND DIP SPICE
Tahini Sauce is the traditional sauce for Falafel Sandwiches. It is easily prepared to perfection each time with this blend. Also use it in Fresh Tomato and Cucumber Salad, Ful Mudammas (Egyptian Fava Bean Salad) and other dishes.

Ingredients: Salt, Garlic, Lemon Juice Powder, Citric, Spices (Coriander, Cumin, Black Pepper and others), Onion, Cornstarch, Calcium Phosphate (prevents caking).

SHAFIK'S RED LENTIL SOUP SPICE
The author developed this blend for her husband, Shafik, who wanted Red Lentil Soup like his mother used to make. Use it to make Bulgur Pilaf and sprinkle it on steamed vegetables. You will be delighted with the well-rounded flavor it adds to our Béchamel Sauce recipe.

Ingredients: Onion, Salt, Spices (Coriander, White Pepper and others), Garlic, Lemon Juice Powder, Cornstarch, Sugar, Citric.

TANDOORI BOMBAY BLEND
Tandoori is traditionally blended with plain yogurt for an unforgettable chicken marinade. Use it in your favorite pilaf recipes and try our recipes for Chicken in Tandoori Almond Sauce and Tandoori Chicken Salad.

Ingredients: Spices (Cardamom, Cloves, Coriander, Ginger, Fenugreek, Nutmeg, Black Pepper, White Pepper and others), Salt, Garlic.

* Salt Free

APPETIZERS

DIPS

◆ Denotes Vegetarian
✤ Denotes Vegan/Lenten

MEDITERRANEAN BLACK BEAN ✤ LAVOSH SWIRLS

Makes 20 swirls

1 15 oz can	black beans
2 Tbsp	chopped parsley
1 Tbsp	finely chopped cilantro
1 Tbsp	extra virgin olive oil
1 1/2 tsp	*SPICE BAZAAR JERUSALEM HUMMUS SPICE*
1/4 cup	diced onion
1/2 cup	diced tomato
2 pieces	12" soft lavosh or flour tortillas

Place the beans in a strainer and rinse well. Drain thoroughly. Transfer the beans to a food processor and add the parsley, cilantro, olive oil and *JERUSALEM HUMMUS SPICE*. Process until fairly smooth. Transfer to a medium bowl and stir in diced tomatoes and onions. Spread half of the mixture on a soft lavosh or flour tortilla to within 1 inch of the edge. Roll up tightly and wrap in plastic wrap. Repeat with the rest of the mixture. Refrigerate overnight. To serve, remove plastic wrap and slice the roll into 1/2 inch slices. Arrange on a platter and sprinkle with additional chopped parsley.

HERBED FRENCH FETA ◆

A platter of Herbed French Feta offers an elegant presentation on appetizer or buffet tables.

1/2 lb	French feta cheese
1 1/2 tsp	*SPICE BAZAAR HERBES DE FRANCE*
1 Tbsp	extra virgin olive oil
1 medium	ripe tomato, diced
1 tsp	chopped parsley
1/4 lb	Calamata olives

Sprinkle 1/2 tsp *HERBES DE FRANCE* on a medium serving dish. Drizzle with 1 tsp olive oil. Cut feta into 1/4 inch slices and place on the dish. Sprinkle with 1 tsp *HERBES DE FRANCE* and top with diced tomato. Drizzle remaining oil on top. Sprinkle with parsley and place Calamata olives around the edge of dish for garnish. Cover and refrigerate for 1 to 2 hours or overnight to allow the flavors to develop.

SPANAKOPITA TRIANGLES ◆
(Filo-wrapped Spinach and Cheese Appetizers)
Makes 40 to 45

3/4 cup   melted Clarified Butter (page 159), divided

Filling:

1 10 oz pkg	frozen chopped spinach, defrosted
1/4 lb	feta cheese, crumbled (about 1 cup)
1/4 cup	small curd cottage cheese or ricotta cheese
1/4 cup	finely diced onion
2 Tbsp	chopped parsley
1	egg
2 tsp	lemon juice
1/8 tsp	nutmeg
2 tsp	*SPICE BAZAAR HELLENIC HERB BLEND*
1/2 lb	12x17" filo dough, defrosted (see Handling Filo Dough, page 161)

Line 2 shallow baking pans with parchment or foil, and drizzle each pan with 2 Tbsp Clarified Butter.

Squeeze water from the spinach. Place in a bowl and add the remaining filling ingredients. Mix well.

Place the filo dough on a cutting board with the wide side facing you. Cut the stack into six equal strips. Work with one stack at a time, keeping the others covered, first with waxed paper and then with a slightly damp towel. Lay one strip of filo on the table and brush lightly with Clarified Butter. Lay another strip on top of the buttered strip. Place 2 tsp filling about 2 inches from the edge closest to you. Fold both strips of filo over on top of the filling. Then begin folding diagonally, like a flag, to form a triangle. Place triangles on the buttered baking pan as you roll them. Brush the tops lightly with Clarified Butter. When all are done, brush the tops of the Spanakopitas with any butter that is left. Bake in a preheated 350-degree oven for 35 to 40 minutes until golden brown.

To Freeze Unbaked Spanakopitas: Layer the triangles in a plastic container, separating the layers with waxed paper. When ready to bake, drizzle 2 Tbsp Clarified Butter on baking pan. Place frozen triangles on pan and bake as above.

NOTE: As a main dish or side dish Spanakopitas may be baked in a pan and cut into squares. See page 64.

TYROPITAS ◆
(Filo-wrapped Cheese Appetizers)
Makes 40 to 45

3/4 cup   melted Clarified Butter (page 159), divided

Filling:

1/3 lb	feta cheese, crumbled (about 1 1/4 cups)
1/4 lb	Monterey jack cheese, grated
1/2 cup	small curd cottage cheese or ricotta cheese
1/4 cup	finely diced onion
1	egg
2 tsp	*SPICE BAZAAR HELLENIC HERB BLEND*
1/2 lb	12x17" filo dough, defrosted (see Handling Filo Dough, page 161)

Place cheeses, onion, egg and *HELLENIC HERB BLEND* in a bowl and mix well.

To roll and bake Tyropitas, follow the procedure in the Spanakopita Triangles recipe (page 4), using the cheese filling instead of the spinach.

KIBBIE BALL APPETIZERS
(Meatballs with Bulgur and Onions)
Makes 30 to 40 balls

1 lb	lean ground beef or lamb
1 cup	fine bulgur (#1)*
3/4 cup	water
1 cup	finely minced onion
4 tsp	*SPICE BAZAAR DAMASCUS KIBBIE SPICE*

Preheat oven to 350 degrees. Spray a large shallow baking pan with non-stick spray.

Place all ingredients in a bowl and knead until thoroughly mixed. Let it rest for 5 or 10 minutes until water is absorbed and the mixture stiffens. Shape into 1 inch balls and place in baking pan. Bake for 25 to 35 minutes, until browned. Rotate balls after 15 minutes for even browning.

Serve with Yogurt-Sour Cream Dip (page 14).

*See Glossary of Ingredients page 165.

HOT AND SPICY WINGS

2 lb	chicken wings

1/2 cup	flour
1 1/2 to 2 Tbsp	*SPICE BAZAAR ETHIOPIAN HOT SPICE*
1 1/2 Tbsp	*SPICE BAZAAR RANDA'S SPICE*

4 Tbsp	oil, divided

Preheat oven to 450 degrees. Line a large shallow baking pan with parchment, or use foil and spray with non-stick spray. Drizzle with 2 Tbsp oil.

Rinse wings and leave moist. Remove and discard tips. Cut wings into 2 pieces at the joint. Place flour, *ETHIOPIAN HOT SPICE* and *RANDA'S SPICE* in a plastic bag and shake to mix. Shake the wings, a few at a time, in the flour bag. Place wings on baking pan at least 1/2 inch apart so they will brown well. Drizzle with 2 Tbsp Oil. Bake 35 to 40 minutes until browned, turning once.

HINT: Chicken wings, cleaned and disjointed, can be purchased frozen in 5 lb bags for quick and easy preparation. Defrost the wings before preparing.

KEFTEDES
(Greek Meatball Appetizers)
Makes 25 to 30

Serve Keftedes with Yogurt-Sour Cream Dip (page 14) at your next party. Try them in your favorite spaghetti sauce in place of your usual meatball recipe.

1 lb	lean ground beef or lamb
1/4 cup	finely chopped parsley
1/2 cup	finely minced onion
1/2 cup	plain bread crumbs
1/4 cup	white wine
1	egg
2 Tbsp	*SPICE BAZAAR HELLENIC HERB BLEND*
1/2 tsp	Salt

Place all ingredients in a bowl and mix thoroughly. Shape into 1 inch balls.

Cooking Method #1: Roll Keftedes in flour and deep fry in hot oil. This is the traditional Greek way of making Keftedes.

Cooking Method #2: Heat 2 Tbsp oil in a non-stick frying pan and cook Keftedes over moderately high heat until browned.

Cooking Method #3: Preheat oven to 375 degrees. Place Keftedes in a baking pan and bake for 20 to 30 minutes, until browned, turning occasionally.

See Keftedes in Wine Sauce (page 115) for a wonderful main dish recipe.

SAMBOOSIKS
(Meat-filled Filo Rolls)
Makes 24 to 26 appetizers or 12 to 14 large rolls

2 Tbsp	pine nuts or slivered almonds
1 Tbsp	Clarified Butter (page 159)
1 lb	lean ground beef or lamb
1 cup	diced onion
2 tsp	*SPICE BAZAAR DAMASCUS KIBBIE SPICE*
1/2 lb	12x17" filo dough, defrosted (see Handling Filo Dough, page 161)
1/2 cup	Clarified Butter, melted (page 159)

Preheat oven to 350 degrees. Line a large shallow baking pan with parchment, or foil and brush with 2 Tbsp of the Clarified Butter.

Sauté pine nuts in 1 Tbsp Clarified Butter until lightly browned. Remove and set aside. Add meat, onion and *DAMASCUS KIBBIE SPICE* to the pan and cook until meat is no longer pink and begins to brown. Remove from heat and stir in pine nuts.

Place the filo dough on a cutting board with the narrow side facing you. Cut the stack in half down the middle lengthwise and again down the middle widthwise to make four stacks of dough. Work with one stack at a time, keeping the others covered, first with waxed paper or parchment and then with a slightly damp towel.

Transfer one sheet of filo to the table with the narrow side facing you. Brush lightly with Clarified Butter. Lay another sheet on top. Place 1 Tbsp filling 1 inch up from the bottom edge of dough. Fold the 1 inch of filo over the filling, then fold side edges in. Brush folded edges lightly with Clarified Butter and roll to the end. Place roll, seam side down, on the baking pan. Repeat brushing, filling and rolling procedure with the rest of the dough. Brush the tops with additional Clarified Butter. The rolls will puff up when baked, so do not crowd on the baking pan. Bake 35 to 40 minutes until nicely browned.

For large Samboosiks, lay the 1/2 lb of filo on the table with the wide side facing you and cut the stack in half. Use 2 Tbsp filling in each and roll as for small Samboosiks. Large samboosiks are an excellent choice for an elegant luncheon. Serve with a Greek Salad (page 29) and Zucchini and Onion Sauté (page 68).

MUHAMMARA ✤
(Roasted Red Pepper and Walnut Dip)
Makes 3 cups

Muhammara is served as a condiment with grilled meats and chicken. It is also great as a dip or a sandwich spread.

1 1/2 cups	walnuts
1 16 oz jar	roasted red peppers
1/3 cup	hot pepper paste* OR 1 Tbsp concentrated hot pepper paste
1/2 cup	plain bread crumbs
1 Tbsp	pomegranate syrup*
2 Tbsp	olive oil
2 tsp	Aleppo pepper* or hot chile
2 tsp	SPICE BAZAAR SESAME TAHINI SAUCE AND DIP SPICE

Place walnuts in a food processor and process until finely chopped. Drain roasted red peppers, reserving liquid. Place in the processor with remaining ingredients. Process until almost smooth, adding reserved red pepper liquid and a little water if needed to obtain a dip consistency.

Variation: For a mellower Muhammara, blend it into 8 oz of softened cream cheese.

NOTE: The hot pepper paste is preferred in this recipe. However, the concentrated paste, which is available in supermarkets, may be used.

*See Glossary of Ingredients pages 165-167.

FRENCH ARTICHOKE DIP ◆
Makes 2 cups

1 14 oz can	artichoke hearts in water
1/2 cup	sour cream
1/2 cup	mayonnaise
1/4 cup	grated Parmesan cheese
2 tsp	SPICE BAZAAR HERBES DE FRANCE
1/4 tsp	salt

Drain and chop artichokes. Mix with the remaining ingredients and refrigerate 2 to 3 hours before serving.

Variation: Place dip in a small baking dish. Sprinkle with additional 1/4 cup grated Parmesan cheese. Place under a preheated broiler for 5 minutes until golden brown. Serve immediately.

HUMMUS ✤
(Chick Pea and Tahini Dip)
Makes 2 cups

Hummus, the most popular dip in the Middle East, is a "must" at every dinner and gathering where food is served. *JERUSALEM HUMMUS SPICE* contains the perfect balance of garlic and lemon to give consistently delicious results every time. High in protein, Hummus makes a great snack with pita bread or fresh vegetables.

1 15 oz can	garbanzo beans
1/3 cup	sesame tahini paste*
2 tsp	*SPICE BAZAAR JERUSALEM HUMMUS SPICE*
	olive oil, paprika and chopped parsley for garnish

Drain garbanzos, reserving the bean juice. Place in a food processor or blender with 1/2 cup of the juice and process until smooth. Transfer the pureed beans to a bowl. Add the sesame tahini paste and *JERUSALEM HUMMUS SPICE* and mix well. If the Hummus is too stiff, add a little more bean juice or water. Spread on a shallow serving dish, drizzle with olive oil, sprinkle with paprika and garnish with chopped parsley.

To add extra zip to your Hummus, substitute *SPICE BAZAAR ETHIOPIAN HOT SPICE* for the paprika. Hummus freezes well for up to 3 months, so prepare an extra batch for your next party or barbecue.

*See Glossary of Ingredients page 167.

BABA GANOUJ ❖
(Eggplant and Tahini Dip)
Makes 1 1/2 to 2 cups

The traditional way to make Baba Ganouj is over a charcoal grill. This gives the dip a delicious smoky flavor. In this recipe the eggplant is broiled until charred. If desired, 1 to 2 drops of liquid smoke can be added to enhance the smoky flavor.

1 large	eggplant
1/3 to 1/2 cup	sesame tahini paste*
1 to 2 cloves	garlic, crushed
1 to 2 Tbsp	*SPICE BAZAAR SESAME TAHINI SAUCE AND DIP SPICE*
1 to 2 drops	liquid smoke (optional)

Chopped parsley, pomegranate seeds (optional) and olive oil for garnish

Preheat oven to broil.

Prick eggplant several times and place on a foil lined baking tray. Broil until the skin is charred, turning as needed to char evenly. This should take 20 to 30 minutes. When cool enough to handle, peel off the skin and place the pulp in a medium bowl. Mash with a fork or potato masher. There should be about 1 1/4 cups of eggplant. If there is more or less than this, adjust quantities of the other ingredients accordingly.

Stir in the sesame tahini paste, garlic, and *SESAME TAHINI SAUCE AND DIP SPICE*. If a smokier flavor is desired, add the liquid smoke. Chill thoroughly. When ready to serve, spread the Baba Ganouj on a shallow serving dish. Garnish with chopped parsley and pomegranate seeds and drizzle with olive oil. Serve with pita bread wedges and fresh vegetables for dipping.

Baba Ganouj freezes well for up to 3 months.

NOTE: It is always best to buy fresh eggplant that is smooth and firm and use it soon after purchasing. It's flavor will be mild and delicious. As it gets older, it develops a sharp, harsh flavor. If this is the case, add a little more sesame tahini paste to mellow it out. Then add a little more *SESAME TAHINI SAUCE AND DIP SPICE* to taste.

*See Glossary of Ingredients page 167.

ETHIOPIAN BERBERE SAUCE ❖
Makes 1 1/2 cups

As a condiment, this sauce will spark up any meat, poultry or fish recipe. Blend it with softened cream cheese for a zesty dip.

2 to 3	jalapeño peppers, seeded
2	cloves garlic
1/2 cup	dried minced onion
1/2 cup	peanut oil
1 Tbsp	white vinegar
1 Tbsp	lemon juice
1/4 cup	dry red wine
2 tsp	salt
1 1/2 Tbsp	*SPICE BAZAAR ETHIOPIAN HOT SPICE*

Place all the ingredients in a blender and blend until smooth and thick.

NOTE: Jalapeño peppers are very hot. Wash hands immediately after handling or use rubber gloves to protect sensitive hands.

MOROCCAN ONION AND RAISIN CHUTNEY ❖
Makes 2 cups

1 12 to 14 oz	box raisins (about 2 1/4 cups)
1 Tbsp	olive oil
2 cups	diced onion
1 Tbsp	*SPICE BAZAAR MOROCCAN BLEND*
3/4 cup	water
1 Tbsp	vinegar

Place raisins and oil in a food processor and chop coarsely. For easier chopping if the raisins are dry, soak them in warm water for a few minutes. Transfer to a medium saucepan and add the remaining ingredients. Bring to a boil. Reduce heat and simmer, uncovered, for 20 to 30 minutes, until mixture is thick and dark. Stir frequently while cooking, to prevent scorching. Serve warm with meats, poultry and pilafs, or cold as a dip or sandwich spread.

ETHIOPIAN EGGPLANT RELISH ✤
Makes 4 cups

Serve this relish as an accompaniment to broiled meats, fish and poultry, or as a dip with pita bread.

1 large	eggplant
1/4 cup	olive oil
2	cloves garlic, crushed
1/2 cup	diced celery
1	long green chile pepper, seeded and chopped
1/2 cup	chopped parsley
1 8 oz can	tomato sauce
1 Tbsp	sugar
1/4 cup	red wine vinegar
1 Tbsp	*SPICE BAZAAR ETHIOPIAN HOT SPICE*
1/2 tsp	salt

Dice eggplant into 1/4 inch cubes. Heat oil in a large, deep frying pan and sauté eggplant over moderately high heat until golden brown. Add the remaining ingredients and simmer, covered, for 10 minutes. Uncover and simmer 10 minutes longer, until mixture is thick and vegetables are soft. May be served warm or cold.

See Ethiopian Eggplant and Shrimp (page 89) for a hearty and flavorful main dish.

CREAMY GREEK DRESSING AND DIP ◆
Makes 1 1/4 to 1 1/2 cups

1 cup	sour cream
1 Tbsp	wine vinegar
1 Tbsp	extra virgin olive oil
1 1/2 tsp	anchovy paste
1 Tbsp	*SPICE BAZAAR GREEK SALAD DRESSING BLEND*

To prepare the dip, place all ingredients in a small bowl and mix well.

For a delicious salad dressing, blend in 2 to 4 Tbsp milk to thin to dressing consistency.

CREAMY GARLIC DRESSING AND DIP ◆
Makes 2 to 2 1/2 cups

This is a great dip to serve with Hot and Spicy Chicken Wings (page 6) or fresh vegetables and chips.

1 cup	sour cream
1/2 cup	mayonnaise
2 Tbsp	lemon juice
1/4 cup	olive oil
4	cloves garlic, crushed
2 Tbsp	*SPICE BAZAAR EGYPTIAN LENTIL SOUP SPICE*

To prepare the dip, place all the ingredients in a small bowl and mix well.

To prepare as a dressing, thin the dip with 1/4 to 1/2 cup milk.

YOGURT-SOUR CREAM DRESSING AND DIP ◆
Makes 2 1/4 cups

Yogurt-Sour Cream Dressing and Dip is a perfect complement to Chicken Gyros (page 80). It also makes a terrific spread for cold cuts or cheese sandwiches. Use it instead of Ranch Dip for fresh vegetables and chips.

1 cup	sour cream
1 cup	plain yogurt
1/4 cup	mayonnaise
1 Tbsp	*SPICE BAZAAR HELLENIC HERB BLEND*

To prepare the dip, place all the ingredients in a bowl and mix well.
Too prepare as a dressing, thin with 2 to 4 Tbsp milk.

SOUPS

SALADS & DRESSINGS

◆ Denotes Vegetarian
❖ Denotes Vegan/Lenten

ATHENIAN GARDEN VEGETABLE SOUP ✣
Makes 12 cups

ATHENIAN GARDEN SPICE gives this vegetable soup a full flavor and satisfying richness that will please even the most determined meat eater.

1 medium	onion, cut into chunks
3 Tbsp	olive oil
1/4 cup	celery chunks
1	carrot, peeled and cut into 1/4 inch slices
1 cup	canned garbanzos or other beans, with juice
1 15 oz can	crushed tomatoes
1/2 cup	barley or shelled whole wheat*
3 Tbsp	*SPICE BAZAAR ATHENIAN GARDEN SPICE*
8 cups	water
1/4 cup	frozen or fresh green beans
1/4 cup	peas
1/4 cup	broccoli
1 small	potato, diced

In a 6 quart pot, sauté the onion in olive oil until lightly browned. Add the celery, carrot, beans with juice, tomatoes, barley or wheat, *ATHENIAN GARDEN SPICE* and water. Simmer, covered, until the barley or wheat is almost tender, 30 to 40 minutes. Add the remaining vegetables and simmer 15 minutes more or until the potatoes are done.

NOTE: Vegetables may be varied as desired.

*See Glossary of Ingredients page 167.

EGYPTIAN LENTIL SOUP ✤
Makes 6 cups

1 cup	diced celery
1 cup	diced onion
2 Tbsp	olive oil

1 cup	brown lentils, rinsed
8 cups	water
2 Tbsp	*SPICE BAZAAR EGYPTIAN LENTIL SOUP SPICE*
2 cups	cut up greens (spinach, kale or collard), optional

In a 4 quart pot, sauté celery and onion in olive oil until onion is very brown. Add lentils, water and *EGYPTIAN LENTIL SOUP SPICE*. Bring to a boil. Reduce heat and simmer, covered, 30 to 40 minutes, until soup is thick and the lentils are tender. If using greens, add them during the last 15 minutes

SHAFIK'S RED LENTIL SOUP ✤
Makes 6 cups

Red lentils can be found in Middle Eastern or Indian grocery stores and in gourmet and health food stores. This soup is so delicious and easy to make that it is worth going out of your way to find the red lentils. It can also be prepared with yellow split peas.

1 cup	finely diced celery
1/2 cup	diced onion
2 Tbsp	olive oil

1 cup	red lentils, rinsed
1	medium carrot, chopped or grated
1 Tbsp	*SPICE BAZAAR SHAFIK'S RED LENTIL SOUP SPICE*

| 6 cups | water |

| 1 Tbsp | chopped parsley |

In a 4 quart pot, sauté celery and onion in olive oil until onion is browned. Add the red lentils, carrots, *SHAFIK'S RED LENTIL SOUP SPICE* and water and bring to a boil. Reduce heat and simmer, covered, 1 hour or until red lentils are tender and soup is thick. Add more water if thinner soup is desired, or cook a little longer for thicker soup. Stir in the chopped parsley before serving.

Serve Shafik's Red Lentil Soup with Feta and Herb Bread (page 120) and a crisp green salad with Herbed French Vinaigrette (page 26).

RICH WHITE BEAN AND TOMATO SOUP ❖
Makes 6 cups

1 cup	diced celery
1 1/2 cups	diced onion
1	clove garlic, crushed
2 tsp	SPICE BAZAAR GARAM MASALA INDIAN BLEND
3 Tbsp	olive oil
3 15 oz cans	white beans, with juice
1 cup	canned crushed tomatoes
2 cups	water
1 tsp	salt
1 Tbsp	lemon juice

In a 4 quart pot, sauté celery, onion, garlic and *GARAM MASALA INDIAN BLEND* in olive oil until onion is browned. Add beans with juice, tomatoes, water and salt and bring to a boil. Reduce heat and simmer, covered, for 20 minutes. Add more water if soup is too thick or simmer longer if too thin. Stir in lemon juice when done.

For Dried Beans: Cook one cup dried beans according to package directions. Follow procedure above, substituting the cooked beans and cooking water for the canned beans and juice. Adjust water quantity as needed.

SPICY SPLIT PEA SOUP ❖
Makes 10 to 12 cups

2 cups	diced celery
1 cup	diced onion
1/4 cup	olive oil
2 cups	green split peas, rinsed
2 small	carrots, chopped or grated
1/4 cup	chopped cilantro
1 tsp	baking soda
4 tsp	SPICE BAZAAR JERICHO FALAFEL SPICE
2 Tbsp	SPICE BAZAAR ATHENIAN GARDEN SPICE
2 Tbsp	lemon juice
3 qts	water

In a 6 quart pot, sauté celery and onion in oil until onion is browned. Add the remaining ingredients and bring to a boil. Reduce heat and simmer, covered, for 1 1/2 hours or until peas are tender and soup is thick. Add more water if soup is too thick or simmer longer if too thin.

AVGOLEMONO SOUP
(Greek Egg-lemon Soup with Chicken)
Makes 10 cups

This is the most popular Greek soup. Its richness and lemony flavor is very satisfying and is a wonderful addition to any Greek meal.

2/3 cup	finely diced onion
1/2 cup	finely diced celery
2 Tbsp	Clarified Butter (page 159) or olive oil

6 cups	chicken broth
1/2 cup	calrose (pearl or medium grain) rice
2 small	carrots, finely chopped or grated
8 oz	boneless, skinless chicken breast, rinsed and diced
1 tsp	SPICE BAZAAR JERUSALEM HUMMUS SPICE
	Salt to taste

1 recipe	Avgolemono Sauce (page 21)

In a 4 quart pot, sauté onion and celery in Clarified Butter or oil until onion is browned. Add broth, rice, carrots, chicken and *JERUSALEM HUMMUS SPICE*. Bring to a boil. Reduce heat and simmer, covered, 15 minutes until rice is tender.

Meanwhile, prepare Avgolemono Sauce. When rice is tender, pour Avgolemono Sauce slowly into soup, whisking continuously. Simmer 10 minutes longer.

TARATORI SOUP ◆
(Greek Cold Yogurt and Cucumber Soup)
Makes about 6 cups

This cold soup is especially refreshing on warm summer days. It's great as a light snack or with a sandwich for lunch.

1 small	cucumber, seeded and grated (about 1 cup)
4 cups	yogurt
1 tsp	crushed garlic
1 tsp	dried or 1 Tbsp fresh chopped mint
1/2 tsp	dried dill
1 Tbsp	SPICE BAZAAR ATHENIAN GARDEN SPICE
1/2 cup	milk
	water to thin

Mix all ingredients in a large bowl. Add water as needed to thin to the consistency of buttermilk. Serve cold.

AVGOLEMONO SAUCE ◆
(Greek Egg-lemon Sauce)
Makes 4 cups

1/4 cup	butter
1/4 cup	flour
2 cups	chicken broth or vegetable broth
1 cup	milk
4	eggs
1 Tbsp	*SPICE BAZAAR JERUSALEM HUMMUS SPICE*
2 Tbsp	lemon juice

In a medium saucepan, melt butter over medium heat. Add flour and stir briskly until bubbly and color begins to deepen slightly. Slowly add broth and milk, whisking continuously until mixture comes to a boil and thickens. Remove from heat and set aside.

In a medium bowl, vigorously whisk eggs and *JERUSALEM HUMMUS SPICE* together until thick and foamy. Pour beaten eggs into flour and broth mixture in a slow, steady stream, whisking continuously. Return saucepan to medium heat and continue stirring and cooking until sauce comes to a boil and thickens. Stir in lemon juice.

MOROCCAN CHICKEN SOUP
Makes 8 cups

Let the soothing aroma of this quick and easy Moroccan Chicken Soup waft through your home and draw everyone to the table. It is especially appreciated for those "under the weather" days.

2 cups	diced celery
1 cup	diced onion
2 Tbsp	Clarified Butter (page 159) or olive oil
3/4 lb	boneless skinless chicken breasts or thighs, rinsed and diced
2	carrots, peeled and cut into 1/4 inch slices
1/4 cup	chopped parsley
1/3 cup	parboiled rice (Uncle Ben's®)
4 15 oz cans	low salt chicken broth
1 Tbsp	*SPICE BAZAAR MOROCCAN BLEND*
2 Tbsp	lemon juice

In a 4 quart pot, sauté the diced celery and onion in the olive oil until the onion is browned. Add the remaining ingredients, *except the lemon juice*, and bring to a boil. Reduce heat and simmer, covered, for 25 to 35 minutes. Turn off heat and stir in the lemon juice.

Serve a bowl of hot Moroccan Chicken Soup with Ful Mudammas (page 27) and toasted pita bread for a delicious light meal.

TABOULI ✤
(Parsley and Wheat Salad)
Makes 6 cups

Tabouli is the Queen of Salads in the Middle East. It graces the tables of the most elegant dinners and is always requested at family gatherings. This recipe takes the guesswork out of preparation. A sharp knife or a food processor with a sharp blade makes quick work of the chopping.

1/2 cup	medium bulgur (#2)*
1/2 cup	lemon juice
4 large	bunches parsley (or parsley to equal 4 cups chopped)
2 medium	tomatoes, diced
1 small	cucumber, peeled and diced
1/2 cup	diced onion
1 Tbsp	dried mint or 1/4 cup chopped fresh mint
1 tsp	salt
1/2 tsp	pepper
1/4 tsp	SPICE BAZAAR MIDDLE EASTERN BLEND
1/4 cup	extra virgin olive oil

Place bulgur in a large bowl and stir in the lemon juice. Set aside while preparing the vegetables so bulgur will absorb the lemon juice.

Rinse and prepare parsley as directed on page 163 (#10 Parsley). Chop parsley very fine. If using a food processor, chop small batches of parsley at a time. Pulse rapidly and do not over-process.

Place parsley in the bowl with the soaked bulgur. Add remaining ingredients and toss to mix. Refrigerate for one hour until the bulgur is softened.

NOTE: The bulgur and vegetables, *except the onions*, may be prepared up to one day in advance. When ready to serve, add the diced onions, seasonings and oil and toss.

*Fine bulgur (#1) may be substituted. See Glossary of Ingredients page 165.

FATTOUSH ✢
(Middle Eastern Salad with Pita Croutons)
Makes 4 to 6 servings

This hearty salad is popular throughout the Middle East and makes good use of leftover pita bread.

2 cups	coarsely chopped romaine lettuce
1	cucumber, peeled, quartered lengthwise and sliced 1/4 inch thick
1 small	green bell pepper, seeded and chopped
4	whole green onions, coarsely chopped
2 medium	tomatoes, coarsely chopped
1/2 cup	parsley, finely chopped
2	pita breads, toasted and broken into bite size pieces
1 recipe	Syrian Salad Dressing (below)

Place vegetables in a salad bowl and add the toasted pita pieces.
Pour dressing over salad and toss.

SYRIAN SALAD DRESSING ✢
Makes 1 cup

1/4 cup	lemon juice
1/4 cup	water
1/2 cup	extra virgin olive oil
1	clove garlic, crushed
2 tsp	dried mint or 2 Tbsp chopped fresh mint
1 Tbsp	*SPICE BAZAAR SESAME TAHINI SAUCE AND DIP SPICE*
2 tsp	sumac*

Place all the ingredients in a small bowl and whisk until thick.

*See Glossary of Ingredients page 167.

FRESH TOMATO AND CUCUMBER SALAD ✣
Makes 4 cups

1 medium	cucumber, peeled and diced
2 medium	tomatoes, diced
1/4 cup	diced onion
1/4 cup	chopped parsley
2 tsp	dried mint or 2 Tbsp chopped fresh mint
3 Tbsp	extra virgin olive oil
2 tsp	SPICE BAZAAR SESEME TAHINI SAUCE AND DIP SPICE

Prepare vegetables and mix in the mint, olive oil and SESAME TAHINI SAUCE AND DIP SPICE. Salad may be prepared ahead and actually improves in flavor after one to two hours.

TAHINI SALAD ✣
(Tomato and Cucumber Salad in Tahini Dressing)
Makes 3 to 4 cups

This saucy salad is a favorite throughout the Middle East. It is a perfect accompaniment to broiled meats and fish. It is often served on Falafel sandwiches.

Tahini Dressing:

1/4 cup	sesame tahini paste*
1/4 cup	water
2 tsp	SPICE BAZAAR SESAME TAHINI SAUCE AND DIP SPICE

Vegetables:

1 medium	cucumber, peeled and diced
2 medium	tomatoes, diced
1/4 cup	diced onion
1/4 cup	chopped parsley

In a medium bowl blend the dressing ingredients until smooth. Add the vegetables and mix. Leftover salad keeps well and even improves in flavor the next day.

*See Glossary of Ingredients page 167.

SPINACH SALAD WITH DRIED CRANBERRIES AND BLEU CHEESE ◆
Makes 8 servings

Try this salad for the holidays. The presentation and flavors are very festive.

2 pkg	fresh baby spinach (6 oz each)
1/2 cup	crumbled bleu cheese
1/2 cup	dried cranberries
1/2 cup	pecans, lightly toasted and coarsely chopped
1 cup	Herbed French Vinaigrette (below)

Divide spinach equally between 8 salad plates. Top each salad with 1 Tbsp each bleu cheese, dried cranberries and pecans. Drizzle 2 Tbsp Herbed French Vinaigrette over each salad.

NOTE: If refrigerator space permits, salads may be assembled ahead. Loosely cover with plastic wrap and keep chilled. Add dressing just before serving.

HERBED FRENCH VINAIGRETTE ✿
Makes 1 2/3 cups

1/2 cup	extra virgin olive oil
1/2 cup	salad oil
1/3 cup	balsamic vinegar
1/3 cup	lemon juice
1 1/2 Tbsp	*SPICE BAZAAR HERBES DE FRANCE*
1 tsp	sugar
1 tsp	salt
1/2 tsp	pepper

Place all the ingredients in a small bowl and whisk until thick.

This dressing is great over fresh greens and is used in the Steak and Pasta Salad recipe on page 33.

SPINACH SALAD WITH LEBANESE DRESSING ❖
Makes 4 servings

16 oz pkg	fresh baby spinach
1/2 medium	red bell pepper, thinly sliced
1/2 cup	thinly sliced red onion
1 cup	sliced mushrooms
1 recipe	Lebanese Salad Dressing (below)

Place spinach in a bowl with the red pepper, onion and mushrooms. Pour Lebanese Salad Dressing over vegetables and toss to coat.

LEBANESE SALAD DRESSING ❖
Makes 2/3 cup

1/4 cup	extra virgin olive oil
2 Tbsp	balsamic vinegar
1/4 cup	water
1 clove	garlic, crushed
2 tsp	SPICE BAZAAR LEBANESE KIFTA SPICE

Place all the ingredients in a small bowl and whisk until thick. This dressing also is great on mixed greens, and makes an excellent marinade for chilled cooked vegetables.

FUL MUDAMMAS ❖
(Egyptian Fava Bean Salad)
Makes 2 cups

Ful Mudammas is part of the daily diet in Egypt. It is often served warm for breakfast with olive oil drizzled on top.

1 15 oz can	fava beans* (or other beans of your choice)
1/3 cup	diced onion
1/3 cup	diced tomato
1/3 cup	chopped parsley
1 Tbsp	pomegranate syrup* (optional, but it really adds to the flavor)
2 Tbsp	extra virgin olive oil
1 Tbsp	SPICE BAZAAR SESAME TAHINI SAUCE AND DIP SPICE

Drain fava beans into a strainer, reserving liquid. Rinse beans and place in a bowl. Mix in the remaining ingredients, adding enough of the reserved liquid to make a saucy bean salad.

Serve with pita bread for dipping in the flavorful salad juices.

*See Glossary of Ingredients page 165 & 166.

TSATSIKI ◆
(Yogurt and Cucumber Salad with Garlic and Mint)
Makes 2 cups

2 cups	plain yogurt
2 medium	cucumbers, peeled and diced
1 tsp	salt
1 clove	garlic, crushed
1 tsp	dried mint or 2 Tbsp chopped fresh mint
1 tsp	*SPICE BAZAAR ATHENIAN GARDEN SPICE*

Line a strainer with a double layer of cheesecloth or paper towels and set in a bowl. Place the yogurt in the strainer for 30 minutes to drain off excess liquid*. Meanwhile, place the cucumbers in another strainer or a colander and sprinkle with salt. Set the strainer in a bowl to drain for 30 minutes. Then gently press the cucumbers to remove more water. Place drained yogurt in a bowl and mix in the cucumbers, garlic, mint and *ATHENIAN GARDEN SPICE*.

*Some brands of yogurt may not drain well because of the gelatin or other ingredients that they contain. With these yogurts, the result will be a thinner Tsatsiki.

RAITA ◆
(Indian Yogurt and Cucumber Sauce)
Makes 2 cups

Raita is the cooling cucumber sauce that is served with hot dishes in Indian restaurants.

1 medium	cucumber, peeled, seeded and grated
1 tsp	salt
2 cups	yogurt
1 clove	garlic, crushed
1 tsp	*SPICE BAZAAR GARAM MASALA INDIAN BLEND*

Place the grated cucumber in a strainer and sprinkle with salt. Set the strainer in a bowl to drain for 30 minutes. Then gently press the cucumber to remove more water. Transfer to a bowl and stir in the yogurt, garlic and *GARAM MASALA INDIAN BLEND*.

GREEK SALAD ◆

Makes 6 servings

This hearty salad is a welcome addition to buffet and appetizer tables. To make a lighter salad, add more romaine or other lettuce.

1/2 head	romaine, cut up
1	cucumber, peeled and sliced
1	tomato, cut into wedges
1 cup	sliced red onion
1/2	each, green, red and yellow bell peppers, seeded and sliced
1/2 cup	Greek peppers (pepperoncinis)
1/4 cup	chopped parsley
1/4 lb	feta cheese, crumbled or cubed (1 cup)
2	celery ribs, sliced into 1/2 inch pieces
1 cup	sliced mushrooms
1/2 lb	Calamata olives
1/2 cup	Greek Salad Dressing (below)
	anchovy filets for garnish (optional)

Place all salad ingredients, *except anchovies*, in a bowl. Pour dressing over salad and toss. Garnish with anchovy filets.

NOTE: For milder and less salty anchovies, soak in milk several hours or overnight. Keep refrigerated until ready to serve.

GREEK SALAD DRESSING ✤

Makes 2 cups

1/2 cup	extra virgin olive oil
1/2 cup	salad oil
1/4 cup	red wine vinegar
2 Tbsp	white vinegar
1/2 cup	water
2 Tbsp	*SPICE BAZAAR GREEK SALAD DRESSING BLEND*
1 clove	garlic, crushed

Place all ingredients in a bowl and whisk until thick.

MOROCCAN COUSCOUS SALAD ❖

Makes 4 cups

1 1/4 cups	water
1/4 cup	olive oil
2 tsp	SPICE BAZAAR MOROCCAN BLEND
1 cup	couscous
5 or 6	Calamata olives, pitted and quartered
1/2 cup	frozen peas, defrosted
1/4 cup	chopped parsley
1/4 cup	diced red pepper
2 Tbsp	currants
1/2 cup	canned garbanzo beans, drained

Place water, olive oil and MOROCCAN BLEND in a medium saucepan.
Bring to a boil and stir in the couscous. Cover and turn off heat. Let it
sit for about 10 minutes until water is absorbed. Stir lightly with a fork
to fluff and let it cool, uncovered, for several minutes. Meanwhile, place
the remaining ingredients in a medium bowl. When the couscous is
ready, add it to the bowl and toss to mix. Moroccan Couscous Salad may
be served at room temperature or cold.

SYRIAN POTATO SALAD ❖

Makes 6 cups

2 lb	white rose or red potatoes, scrubbed well
1/4 lb	frozen green beans (regular or French cut)
1/2 cup	chopped parsley
2/3 cup	diced onion
1/4 cup	extra virgin olive oil
1 clove	garlic, crushed
1/4 cup	lemon juice
1 Tbsp	SPICE BAZAAR ATHENIAN GARDEN SPICE

Cut potatoes into 1/2 inch cubes. Boil in water to cover, until done but
firm. Drain and transfer to a large bowl. Blanch green beans briefly in
boiling water. Drain and add to potatoes with remaining ingredients and
mix gently. Refrigerate several hours or overnight so flavors will develop.

PARTHENON PASTA SALAD ◆

Makes 8 cups

8 oz	rotini pasta

1 cup	broccoli florets
1/2 cup	sliced fresh mushrooms
1/4 cup	chopped parsley
1/2 cup	diced red pepper
1	rib celery, cut into 1/4 inch slices
1/2 cup	thinly sliced red onions
1 cup	canned garbanzo beans, drained
1/4 cup	cut up Greek peppers (pepperoncinis)
1/4 lb	Calamata olives
1/2 lb	feta cheese, crumbled (about 2 cups)
1 6 oz jar	marinated artichoke hearts

3/4 cup	Greek Salad Dressing (page 29), divided

Cook pasta according to package directions. Drain in a colander and
rinse under cold water. Place in a large bowl. Place broccoli florets in
a strainer and rinse under very hot water until they turn bright green.
Add to pasta with the remaining ingredients, *except Greek Salad
Dressing*. Add 1/4 cup dressing, reserving the rest to add before
serving. Toss lightly. Refrigerate until ready to serve. Before serving,
mix in the rest of the dressing.

SHRIMP AND PASTA SALAD WITH CREAMY GARLIC DRESSING ◆

Makes 12 cups

This pasta salad is a great crowd pleaser. It is economical to make and can be prepared ahead.

12 oz	small shell pasta
1/4 cup	sliced black olives
1/4 cup	chopped parsley
1/2 cup	diced onion
1 clove	garlic, crushed
1/2 cup	thinly sliced red pepper
1 cup	sliced fresh mushrooms
2	ribs celery, sliced
1/2 lb	cooked baby shrimp
1 1/2 to 2 cups	Creamy Garlic Dressing (page 14), divided

Cook pasta according to package directions. Drain in a colander and rinse under cold water. Place in a large bowl. Add the remaining ingredients, *except shrimp and dressing*. Stir in 1 cup dressing, reserving the rest to add before serving. Chill several hours or overnight. When ready to serve, mix in shrimp and 1/2 to 1 cup more dressing.

Serve on a bed of lettuce and accompany with Feta and Herb Bread (page 120).

STEAK AND PASTA SALAD
Makes 8 to 10 cups

This salad is equally delicious served slightly warm or served cold. It makes an attractive and hearty luncheon salad, arranged on romaine or red leaf lettuce. Serve with a loaf of crusty French bread and whipped butter seasoned with a pinch of *SPICE BAZAAR HERBES DE FRANCE*.

1 lb	top sirloin steak
1 to 1 1/2 cups	Herbed French Vinaigrette, (page 26), divided
8 oz	dry mostaccioli, rotini or penne pasta
1/3 lb	feta cheese, crumbled (about 1 1/4 cup)
2 medium	tomatoes, diced
1 cup	thinly sliced red onion
1/4 cup	chopped parsley
2 small	zucchini, cut into 1/2 inch pieces

Place steak in a 1 gallon zip-lock plastic bag and pour dressing over it. Close bag and place on a plate. Refrigerate 1 to 2 hours or overnight, turning occasionally.

Prepare pasta according to package directions. When pasta is almost al dente, add zucchini to the boiling pasta water and let it cook 2 to 3 minutes until tender crisp. Drain pasta and zucchini in a colander and rinse with cold water. Place in a large bowl. Add feta, tomatoes, red onion, parsley, and 1 cup Herbed French Vinaigrette. Toss to mix.

Grill or broil steak just until pink (do not overcook). Slice thinly across the grain. Add sliced steak and remaining dressing to the pasta bowl and toss lightly. Serve warm, or refrigerate and serve cold.

TANDOORI CHICKEN SALAD
Makes 6 cups

1 1/2 lb	boneless, skinless chicken breasts or thighs, rinsed
2/3 cup	diced onion
1 1/2 cup	diced celery
2/3 cup	frozen peas, defrosted
1/3 cup	pine nuts or slivered almonds, toasted
1/3 cup	currants
1 to 1 1/4 cup	Tandoori Dressing (below)

Simmer chicken breasts or thighs in water to cover until tender and no longer pink, 20 to 30 minutes. Drain and let it cool. Dice chicken into large chunks and place in a bowl. Add remaining ingredients and mix well. Chill thoroughly before serving.

NOTE: For a convenient shortcut, use rotisserie chicken from your supermarket. Remove skin and cut up the required amount of chicken.

TANDOORI DRESSING ◆
Makes 1 1/2 cups

3/4 cup	plain yogurt
3/4 cup	mayonnaise
1 1/2 tsp	*SPICE BAZAAR TANDOORI BOMBAY BLEND*

Blend yogurt, mayonnaise and *TANDOORI BOMBAY BLEND* together in a bowl until smooth.

PILAFS, GRAINS
AND POTATOES

◆ Denotes Vegetarian
✤ Denotes Vegan/Lenten

HASHWEH
(Rice Dressing with Ground Meat)
Makes 4 cups

"Hashweh" is the Arabic word for "stuffing". This is the most popular stuffing for holiday turkey and chicken. The aroma of the spices fills the house and whets the whole family's appetite. It is also served as a side dish with many Middle Eastern dishes.

1/2 lb	lean ground lamb or beef
2 Tbsp	Clarified Butter (page 159)
2 tsp	*SPICE BAZAAR MIDDLE EASTERN BLEND*
1 tsp	salt
1 cup	parboiled rice (Uncle Ben's®)
2 cups	water
1/4 cup	pine nuts or slivered almonds, toasted

As a Side Dish: Place the ground lamb or beef, Clarified Butter, *MIDDLE EASTERN BLEND* and salt in a medium saucepan and brown well. Add rice and stir for 1 minute. Add water and half of the nuts (set the other half aside for garnish). Bring to a boil. Reduce heat and simmer, covered, for 25 minutes or until rice is tender and water is absorbed. Gently stir rice about half way through the cooking. When rice is done, give it another gentle stir. If the rice is sticking to the bottom of the pan, add a couple tablespoons of water. Cover and let it sit for about 10 minutes before serving. The 10-minute rest period allows the rice to firm up so the grains will stay separated. Place Hashweh on a platter and sprinkle with remaining nuts.

As a Turkey or Chicken Stuffing: Prepare as above *except* reduce water to 1 3/4 cups. Cook until water is absorbed, and then stuff the bird.

PERFECT RICE EVERY TIME

Following are general preparation instructions and a chart with proportions of rice to water, etc., for several different varieties of rice. Basmati is a fine flavored rice from India. It is more expensive than other varieties, but cooks up to greater volume. Jasmine rice is from Thailand and has a wonderful, distinctive aroma and flavor. Calrose rice is a medium grain or pearl rice, which is sometimes referred to as "sticky rice". Long grain rice is the most common variety in supermarkets. Parboiled rice, commonly known as Uncle Ben's® Rice, is popular because it is almost foolproof to cook. Whatever variety you choose, always buy the finest quality for the best taste and texture.

General Instructions: For rice that requires rinsing, place in a strainer and hold under hot running water until water runs clear. To cook, place butter or oil in a saucepan and add rice and salt. Sauté over medium heat for 1 minute, until the butter or oil is absorbed. Add water and bring to a boil. Reduce heat and simmer, covered, for the required time or until water is absorbed. Gently stir rice about half way through the cooking. When the rice is done, give it another gentle stir. If the rice is sticking to the bottom of the pan, add a couple tablespoons of water. Cover and let it sit for about 10 minutes before serving. The 10-minute rest period allows the rice to firm up so the grains will stay separated.

NOTE: Salted or unsalted butter may be used. Clarified Butter (page 159) is the preferred choice in most rice recipes because it does not burn when sautéing rice. Oil may be used when preparing vegan meals.

Variations:
1. Use broth instead of water.
2. Add a chicken, beef or vegetable bouillon cube and delete salt.
3. Stir in diced vegetables or bits of cooked meat with the water.
4. Try different *SPICE BAZAAR BLENDS* to vary the flavor.

REFER TO CHART ON OPPOSITE PAGE FOR RICE PROPORTIONS AND COOKING TIMES

RICE PROPOROTIONS AND COOKING TIMES

	Basmati ✤	Calrose ✤	Jasmine ✤	Long Grain ✤	Parboiled ✤
Rice	1 cup	1 cup	1 cup	1 cup	1 cup
Butter or oil	2 Tbsp	2 Tbsp	2 Tbsp	2 Tbsp	2 Tbsp
Salt	1/2 tsp	1/2 tsp	1/2 tsp	1/2 tsp	1/2 tsp
Water	2 cups	1 3/4 cups	1 2/3 cups	1 2/3 cup	2 cups
Rinse Before Cooking	Yes	Yes	No	Yes	No
Cooking Time	15 min	15 min	15 min	20 min	25 min
Sitting Time	10 min	10 min	10 min	10 min	10 min
Yield	4 cups	3 1/2 cup	3 1/2 cup	3 1/2 cup	3 cups

NOTES: These proportions are for cooking plain rice. Measurements in the following recipes may vary if vegetables, meats or other ingredients are cooked with the rice. When preparing more than two cups of rice, the proportion of water needs to be reduced slightly, as there will be less evaporation.

FRAGRANT SAFFRON BASMATI RICE ✤
Makes 4 cups

1 cup	basmati rice
2 Tbsp	Clarified Butter (page 159) or oil
1/2 tsp	salt
2 cups	water
1/2 tsp	saffron

Place saffron threads in a small bowl and pound with the wooden end of a knife handle until powdery. Add 1 Tbsp water and microwave for 20 seconds. Set aside to steep. Place rice in a strainer and rinse under hot running water until water runs clear. Place Clarified Butter or oil in a medium saucepan and add rice and salt. Sauté over medium heat for 1 minute until the butter or oil is absorbed. Add the water and saffron with its liquid and bring to a boil. Reduce heat and simmer, covered, for 15 to 20 minutes until the water is absorbed. Gently stir rice about half way through the cooking. When rice is done, give it another gentle stir. If the rice is sticking to the bottom of the pan, add a couple tablespoons of water. Cover and let it sit for about 10 minutes before serving. This rest period allows the rice to firm up so the grains will stay separated.

SYRIAN RICE ✤
Makes 3 1/2 cups

1/4 cup	orzo (rosamarina)* or fine vermicelli, broken
2 Tbsp	Clarified Butter (page 159) or oil
1 cup	parboiled rice (Uncle Ben's®)
2 1/4 cups	low salt chicken broth or water
1/2 tsp	salt

Place Clarified Butter or oil in a medium saucepan. Add orzo or vermicelli and stir constantly over medium heat until noodles are browned. Watch carefully, as it browns very quickly. Immediately add rice and salt. Stir for 1 minute so butter or oil will be absorbed. Add water and bring to a boil. Reduce heat and simmer, covered, for 20 to 30 minutes or until water is absorbed. Gently stir rice about half way through cooking. When rice is done, give it another gentle stir. If it is sticking to the bottom of the pan, add a couple tablespoons of water. Cover and let it sit for about 10 minutes before serving. This rest period allows the rice to firm up so the grains will stay separated.

For variety, try adding different *SPICE BAZAAR BLENDS* to the rice while cooking. Select a blend to complement your main dish. When using blends, which have salt in them, reduce or omit the salt in the recipe.

*See Glossary of Ingredients page 166.

BENARES PILAO ❖
(Basmati Rice with Vegetables and Beans)
Makes 5 cups

This versatile Indian rice dish can be served as a side dish with chicken or fish. Or add small bits of cooked chicken or meat for a main dish. It is excellent as a vegetarian main dish because the kidney beans provide protein while the rice and vegetables round out the meal.

1 cup	basmati rice
2 Tbsp	Clarified Butter (page 159) or oil
1 3/4 cups	water
1/2 cup	peas
1/2 cup	small broccoli florets
1/2 cup	coarsely chopped carrots
1/2 cup	small cauliflower florets
2 whole	green onions, cut into 1/2 inch pieces
1 cup	canned kidney beans, drained and rinsed
1 Tbsp	*SPICE BAZAAR TANDOORI BOMBAY BLEND*

Place rice in a strainer and rinse under hot water until water runs clear. Heat Clarified Butter or oil in a medium saucepan and add rice. Stir over medium heat 1 minute, until butter or oil is absorbed. Add the remaining ingredients and bring to a boil. Reduce heat and simmer, covered, for 15 to 20 minutes until water is absorbed. Gently stir rice about halfway through the cooking. When rice is done, give it another gentle stir. If rice is sticking to bottom of pan, add a couple tablespoons of water. Cover and let it sit for about 10 minutes before serving. This rest period allows the rice to firm up so the grains will stay separated.

RICE PILAF ✤

Makes 4 cups

1/2 cup	finely diced celery
1/2 cup	finely diced onion
2 Tbsp	Clarified Butter (page 159) or oil
1 cup	parboiled rice (Uncle Ben's®)
2 cups	low salt chicken or vegetable broth, or water
2 tsp	*SPICE BAZAAR ATHENIAN GARDEN SPICE*

In a medium saucepan, sauté celery and onion in butter or oil until lightly browned. Add rice and *ATHENIAN GARDEN SPICE* and stir for 1 minute. Add water or broth and bring to a boil. Reduce heat and simmer, covered, for 30 minutes, or until water is absorbed and rice is tender. Gently stir rice about half way through the cooking. When rice is done, give it another gentle stir. If it is sticking to the bottom of the pan, add a couple tablespoons of water. Cover and let it sit for about 10 minutes before serving. This rest period allows the rice to firm up so the grains will stay separated.

Try different *SPICE BAZAAR BLENDS* in this basic Pilaf recipe. Select the blend that will complement your main dish, letting your imagination be your guide. If the blend you select does not have salt, add 1/2 tsp with the rice.

BULGUR PILAF ✤

Makes 4 cups

Slightly nutty and very flavorful, bulgur pilaf is a unique change of pace from rice or potatoes.

1/2 cup	diced onion
3 Tbsp	Clarified Butter (page 159) or oil
1 cup	coarse bulgur (#3 or #4)*
1 small	tomato, diced
2 cups	low salt chicken or vegetable broth, or water
1 Tbsp	*SPICE BAZAAR SHAFIK'S RED LENTIL SOUP SPICE*

In a medium saucepan, sauté onion in butter or oil until lightly browned. Add remaining ingredients and bring to a boil. Reduce heat and simmer, covered, for 15 minutes. Remove lid and stir gently. Replace lid and continue cooking for 10 minutes more, or until water is absorbed. Turn off heat and let it sit for about 10 minutes before serving.

*See Glossary of Ingredients page 165.

MOROCCAN COUSCOUS PILAF ❖
Makes 3 cups

Prepare Moroccan Couscous Pilaf to serve with the traditional
Moroccan Chicken or Lamb Couscous Platter (pages 76 and 110).
Or serve it as a side dish in place of rice or potatoes.

1/4 cup	butter or oil
1/2 cup	frozen peas (optional)
1 1/4 cups	low salt chicken or vegetable broth, or water
1 1/2 tsp	*SPICE BAZAAR MOROCCAN BLEND*
1 cup	couscous

Place butter, peas, broth or water and *MOROCCAN BLEND* in a medium
saucepan. Bring to a boil and stir in couscous. Cover and turn off heat.
Let it sit for about 10 minutes until water is absorbed. Stir lightly with
a fork to fluff before serving.

ORZO WITH FETA ◆
(Rice-shaped Pasta with Feta)
Makes 4 cups

1 cup	orzo (rosamarina)*
1 Tbsp	oil
1/2 tsp	salt
2 Tbsp	olive oil
1 rib	celery, finely diced
1/2 cup	finely diced onion
2	plum tomatoes, diced
1/3 cup	frozen peas
1 tsp	*SPICE BAZAAR HELLENIC HERB BLEND*
1 1/2 tsp	*SPICE BAZAAR ATHENIAN GARDEN SPICE*
1/4 lb	feta cheese, crumbled (about 1 cup)

Bring 2 quarts water to a boil. Add the orzo, 1 Tbsp oil and the salt.
Cook until al dente, about 10 to 12 minutes. Drain and rinse in cold
water. Transfer to a bowl.

While the orzo is cooking, heat 2 tbsp olive oil in a medium frying pan.
Add the celery and onions and sauté until lightly browned. Stir in the
tomatoes, peas and spices. Cook over medium heat for one minute.
Add the vegetables and feta to the orzo and stir in. May be served hot
or cold.

*See Glossary of Ingredients page 166.

IMJADARA WITH RICE ✤
(Lentil and Rice Pilaf)
Makes 4 cups

In Middle Eastern families, this nutritious and homey meal is one of the first thing college kids ask for when returning home. It brings back memories of cozy family meals and togetherness.

1 cup	brown lentils, rinsed
2 cups	water

1 cup	diced onion
3 Tbsp	olive oil

1/2 cup	parboiled rice (Uncle Ben's®) or long grain rice
1 cup	water
1 1/2 Tbsp	*SPICE BAZAAR EGYPTIAN LENTIL SOUP SPICE*

1 large	onion, thinly sliced
2 Tbsp	olive oil

1 tsp	sumac* (optional)

Place lentils in a medium saucepan with 2 cups water and bring to a boil. Reduce heat and simmer, covered, 20 to 25 minutes until water is almost all absorbed. Meanwhile, in a medium frying pan, sauté the diced onion in the 3 Tbsp olive oil until **very brown**. When the lentils are ready, add the sautéed onions and oil, rice, 1 cup water and *EGYPTIAN LENTIL SOUP SPICE*. Return to a boil. Reduce heat and simmer, covered, another 20 minutes, until water is absorbed and rice is tender. Let it sit for about 10 minutes before serving.

While the Imjadara is cooking, prepare the sliced onion. Place 2 Tbsp olive oil in a medium frying pan, add the sliced onion and fry over moderately high heat until well browned, about 10 to 15 minutes.

To Serve: Place the Imjadara on a platter, garnish the top with the fried onions and sprinkle with sumac. Imjadara is traditionally served with Tsatsiki (page 28) or plain yogurt and Fresh Tomato and Cucumber Salad (page 25).

*See Glossary of Ingredients page 167.

IMJADARA WITH BULGUR ✤
(Lentil and Bulgur Pilaf)
Makes 4 cups

1/2 cup	brown lentils, rinsed
2 1/4 cups	water, divided
1/2 cup	diced onion
2 Tbsp	olive oil
1/2 cup	coarse bulgur (#3 or #4)*
1 Tbsp	*SPICE BAZAAR SHAFIK'S RED LENTIL SOUP SPICE*

In a medium saucepan, bring lentils and 1 cup water to a boil. Reduce heat and simmer, covered, 20 to 25 minutes until water is almost all absorbed. Meanwhile, in a small frying pan, sauté onion in olive oil until very brown.

When the lentils are ready, add the sautéed onion and oil, bulgur, *SHAFIK'S RED LENTIL SOUP SPICE* and 1 1/4 cups water. Bring to a boil. Reduce heat and simmer, covered, for another 20 to 25 minutes until water is absorbed. Turn off heat and let it sit for about 10 minutes before serving.

For a change of pace, serve Imjadara with Bulgur in place of rice or potatoes with your favorite meat or poultry. For a satisfying meatless meal, serve it accompanied by Greek Salad (page 29) or Tabouli (page 23).

*See Glossary of Ingredients page 165.

GREEK HOME-BAKED POTATOES ❖
Makes 4 to 5 servings

4 medium potatoes

1/2 cup olive oil
3 Tbsp lemon juice
3 Tbsp SPICE BAZAAR GREEK SALAD DRESSING BLEND

Preheat oven to 450 degrees. Line a shallow baking pan with parchment, or use foil and spray with non-stick spray.

Scrub potatoes, cut in half lengthwise and then into thick wedges. In a medium bowl, whisk together oil, lemon juice and GREEK SALAD DRESSING BLEND. Dip potatoes in the bowl and turn to coat all sides. Place on the baking pan skin side down. Bake for 30 to 40 minutes until crispy and brown.

LEBANESE HASH BROWNS ❖
Makes 3 to 4 servings

2 medium potatoes

3 Tbsp butter or oil
1 cup diced onion
2 1/2 Tbsp SPICE BAZAAR LEBANESE KIFTA SPICE
2 tsp SPICE BAZAAR JERICHO FALAFEL SPICE

Scrub potatoes and pat dry. Grate or dice finely. Heat butter or oil in a large, shallow non-stick frying pan. Add potatoes, onion and spices. Cook over medium heat about 10 minutes, turning occasionally, until potatoes are browned.

NOTE: If more potatoes are needed, divide into two pans for better browning.

HOT AND SPICY SHOESTRING FRIES ✤

unseasoned frozen shoestring fries
Spice Bazaar Ethiopian Hot Spice
Spice Bazaar Randa's Spice

Preheat oven to 425 degrees. Line a shallow baking pan with parchment, or use foil and spray with non-stick spray.

Place fries on the baking pan and sprinkle generously with *Ethiopian Hot Spice* and *Randa's Spice*. Turn to coat all sides. Bake 20 to 25 minutes until crispy.

Serve with barbecued meats or chicken. As a snack, serve Hot and Spicy Shoestring Fries (page 47) with Creamy Garlic Dip (page 14).

POTATO AND ONION OMELET ◆

Makes 4 servings

My daughter Mona often prepares this nourishing quick meal for her seven children at the end of a busy day. She varies the recipe by adding diced red bell peppers, tomatoes or whatever bits of vegetables she has on hand. A salad and bread complete the meal.

6	eggs
3 Tbsp	milk
3 Tbsp	butter
1 cup	diced onion
1 cup	sliced mushrooms
2 large	potatoes, scrubbed and sliced 1/4 inch thick

Spice Bazaar Moroccan Blend

In a medium bowl, beat the eggs and milk until frothy. Set aside.

Heat the butter in a large non-stick frying pan and sauté the onions and mushrooms until lightly browned. Remove with a slotted spoon and set aside.

Lightly sprinkle both sides of the potato slices with *Moroccan Blend*. Place slices in the frying pan and brown on both sides over medium-high heat. Distribute the onions and mushrooms over the top of the potatoes and add 2 to 4 Tbsp water. Cover and cook over low heat 10 to 15 minutes, until the potatoes are done. Remove lid and pour the eggs over the potatoes. Sprinkle lightly again with *Moroccan Blend*. Cover and continue cooking over low heat for 10 to 15 minutes until the eggs are set.

47

ORTHODOX CHURCH MEMORIAL WHEAT ☦

Makes 150 to 200 1 1/2 oz servings

This wheat, which is called **AMMAH** or **RAHMEE** in Arabic and **KOLIVA** in Greek, is offered in the Eastern Orthodox Christian Church in memory of a deceased loved one. It can be offered at 9 days, 40 days and for the 1 year Memorial Service. The wheat is blessed by the priest and then served to all attending the service.

Unshelled whole wheat generally takes about 4 hours to cook. The following method shortens the actual cooking time by letting the wheat sit in the hot water.

4 lb	unshelled whole wheat (wheat berries)*
2 lb	walnuts, coarsely chopped
1 lb	white raisins
1 1/4 cups	sugar
3 Tbsp	ground anise
2 Tbsp	ground cinnamon
2 tsp	ground nutmeg
2 tsp	ground cloves
1/4 lb	Jordan (candied) almonds for decorating

Two Days Before the Memorial Service: Rinse wheat and place in a large pot. Add water to fill the pot. Use plenty of water. Bring to a boil. Reduce heat and simmer, covered, for 1 hour. Turn off heat and let it sit, covered, for 3 to 4 hours. Check the wheat. If it is tender and the kernels have opened up, it is done. If not, bring it to a boil again. Turn off heat and let it sit for another 2 to 3 hours. This method takes longer total time, but it eliminates the need to constantly add water as it evaporates and the need to stir frequently to prevent the wheat from sticking to the bottom of the pot.

When the wheat is done, drain it into a large colander and rinse it well under cold running water. Place the colander in a large bowl, cover it with plastic wrap, and place in the refrigerator overnight. The day before the service, mix in the walnuts, raisins, spices and sugar.

Churches have different customs for serving the Memorial Wheat. Some put it in small individual plastic cups or plastic bags, while others prepare one large platter to serve after the Memorial Service. In either case, prepare a small tray about 12 inches in diameter, which will be used during the actual Memorial Service. The top of the tray can be decorated around the edge with Jordan almonds and a cross in the middle. In some traditions a layer of zweiback crumbs is pressed on top and then the crumbs are covered with a thick layer of powdered sugar. The top is then decorated with the Jordan almonds. This should be done just before taking the wheat to church.

*See Glossary of Ingredients page 167.

48

VEGETARIAN MAIN DISHES

*See the PILAFS, GRAINS & POTATOES section for
additional vegetarian main dishes.*

VEGETABLE SIDE DISHES

◆ Denotes Vegetarian
✤ Denotes Vegan/Lenten

POTATO KIBBIE BALLS ✤
Makes 28 to 30 Potato Kibbie Balls

This meatless version of the classic dish, Kibbie is flavorful and satisfying. It is delicious freshly fried and great as a snack, served cold.

Filling:

1/2 cup	pine nuts or slivered almonds
1/4 cup	oil
1 large	onion, diced
1 can	garbanzo beans, drained and coarsely chopped
1/2 tsp	*SPICE BAZAAR DAMASCUS KIBBIE SPICE*

Dough:

1 cup	bulgur #1*
1 cup	water
2 lb	russet potatoes, peeled and cut into 1/2 inch cubes
1 cup	flour
2 tsp	*SPICE BAZAAR DAMASCUS KIBBIE SPICE*

oil for deep-frying

Prepare the Filling: Heat oil in a large frying pan and sauté the pine nuts until lightly browned. Remove and set aside. Add the onions to the oil and sauté until browned. Stir the garbanzos, pine nuts and 1/2 tsp *DAMASCUS KIBBIE SPICE* into the onions. Sauté for one minute. Set aside.

Prepare the Dough: Place the bulgur in a small bowl and stir in the water. Set aside. Boil potatoes in water to cover until done. Drain and mash. Allow to cool. Add the flour, 2 tsp *DAMASCUS KIBBIE SPICE* and the soaked bulgur. Knead together thoroughly.

Shape Potato Kibbie Balls: Divide dough into golf-ball size pieces. Press a large indentation in the center. Fill with 1 Tbsp filling. Close up and form into a football shape. Heat at least 3 inches of oil in a medium saucepan. Drop 4 or 5 Kibbie Balls into the hot oil and fry 3 to 5 minutes, turning with a slotted spoon until browned. Remove and drain on a paper towel lined tray. Repeat until all the Kibbie Balls are fried.

Variation: For those who prefer not to fry, the Kibbie may be baked in a 9x13 inch pan. Drizzle the pan with 2 Tbsp olive oil and press half of the dough evenly in the bottom of the pan. Spread the filling evenly over the layer of dough. Form patties with the rest of the dough and lay them side-by-side on top of the filling. Use bits of the mixture to fill in empty spaces. Smooth over entire pan with wet hands. Drizzle 2 more Tbsp olive oil over the top. Cut into 2 inch squares and then cut diagonally to form triangles. Bake for 40 to 50 minutes until lightly browned. Then broil on high until browned.

*See Glossary of Ingredients page 165.

MEATLESS DOLMADES ⚘
(Stuffed Grape Leaves)

Makes 40 to 50 Dolmades

Meatless Dolmades are popular as a main dish or as part of a large buffet. They are often served cold as an appetizer.

1 cup	calrose (pearl or medium grain) rice, rinsed well and drained
1 cup	water
1 medium	tomato, diced
1/2 cup	diced onion
1/3 cup	chopped parsley
3 Tbsp	olive oil
4 tsp	***Spice Bazaar Athenian Garden Spice***
1 tsp	dried mint or 1 Tbsp chopped fresh mint
1 1/2 Tbsp	lemon juice
1 pint jar	grape leaves
2 Tbsp	olive oil

Prepare Filling: Place rice and water in a small saucepan. Bring to a boil. Reduce heat and simmer, covered, 5 to 10 minutes, until water is absorbed. Transfer to a medium bowl and mix in the remaining ingredients, ***except the grape leaves and 2 Tbsp olive oil.***

Roll Grape Leaves: Drain water from the jar of grape leaves and carefully remove leaves. Unroll each bundle of leaves and cut off stems. Rinse under running warm water. Drain in a colander. Use 3 or 4 leaves to line the bottom of a medium saucepan. Lay several leaves on the table, side-by-side with the smooth, shiny side down and stem end facing you. Place 2 tsp filling in center of each leaf, pressing to about 1 1/2 inches long. Working from stem end, fold leaf up and over filling, then fold sides in and roll up. Continue filling and rolling the rest of the leaves.

Place the rolled grape leaves snugly side by side in the pan, seam side down, layer upon layer. Drizzle 2 Tbsp olive oil over the rolled grape leaves. Lay an inverted plate over the grape leaves to hold them down while cooking. Add water just to the top of the leaves. Bring to a boil. Reduce heat and simmer, covered, for 30 minutes. Uncover and raise heat to a slow boil. Continue cooking until most of the liquid is evaporated, about 10 minutes.

NOTES: When using fresh grape leaves, blanch them first. Add a little salt and lemon juice to the pot while cooking. Cooked Dolmades freeze well and can be reheated in a steamer or microwave.

MEATLESS MALFOOF ✤
(Cabbage Rolls)
Makes 30 to 40 rolls

Filling Ingredients from Meatless Dolmades recipe (page 52)

1 large head	cabbage

1 Tbsp	SPICE BAZAAR ATHENIAN GARDEN SPICE
1 tsp	SPICE BAZAAR JERUSALEM HUMMUS SPICE
2 Tbsp	olive oil

Follow directions in the Meatless Dolmades recipe for preparing the filling.

Prepare Cabbage: Rinse cabbage and remove core. Place in a plastic bag, leaving end open. Place bag on a microwave-safe plate and microwave on high for 5 minutes. Turn and microwave 2 to 3 minutes more until leaves are softened. Carefully remove cabbage from bag (it will be very hot). Rinse under cold water. Separate leaves and cut the thick vein from the center of each leaf. Leave small leaves whole, cut medium leaves in half and large leaves in thirds. Place scraps of cabbage in the bottom of a 4 quart pot. If the inner leaves of the cabbage head are not softened enough, return to microwave for 2 to 3 minutes more, as needed.

Roll Cabbage: Place 1 to 1 1/2 Tbsp filling in the center of each leaf, pressing to about 2 inches long. Fold leaf over the filling, and then fold sides in and roll up. Place rolls snugly side-by-side in the pot, seam side down, layer upon layer.

Sprinkle *ATHENIAN GARDEN SPICE* and *JERUSALEM HUMMUS SPICE* on top of the rolls. Drizzle with olive oil. Add water just to cover the rolls. Place an inverted plate on top of the cabbage rolls to hold them down while cooking. Bring to a boil. Reduce heat and simmer, covered, for 30 minutes. Remove lid and raise heat to a slow boil. Continue cooking until most of the liquid has evaporated, 10 to 15 minutes more.

NOTE: If there is extra filling, prepare stuffed tomatoes to cook with the cabbage rolls. Cut tops off tomatoes and scoop out insides. Fill with rice mixture. Put tops back on tomatoes. Place in the pot with the cabbage rolls.

MEATLESS SHEIKH EL MAHSHI ✤
(Stuffed Eggplant Boats)
Makes 8 to 10 servings

This is the vegetarian version of a very special dish that translates into "The Sheik of Stuffed Dishes." Serve it over Syrian Rice (page 40) and you will be delighted with the satisfying flavor it offers.

Eggplant Boats:

2 large	eggplants
1/4 cup	olive oil
	SPICE BAZAAR RANDA'S SPICE
	SPICE BAZAAR GARAM MASALA INDIAN BLEND

Filling:

3 Tbsp	olive oil
1 medium	zucchini, diced
1 cup	diced onion
5 large	mushrooms, diced
1 tsp	SPICE BAZAAR GARAM MASALA INDIAN BLEND
1/2 tsp	SPICE BAZAAR RANDA'S SPICE
3 Tbsp	pine nuts or slivered almonds, toasted

Sauce:

2 15 oz cans	crushed tomatoes
1 1/2 cups	water
1 1/2 tsp	SPICE BAZAAR GARAM MASALA INDIAN BLEND
1 tsp	SPICE BAZAAR ATHENIAN GARDEN SPICE
1/2 tsp	SPICE BAZAAR RANDA'S SPICE
3 Tbsp	chopped parsley

Preheat oven to 450 degrees.

Prepare Boats: Cut stems off the eggplants. Cut them in half lengthwise and then in half again across the middle. Cut each quarter into 2 or 3 wedges. Brush the cut surfaces with olive oil, sprinkle with *RANDA'S SPICE* and *GARAM MASALA INDIAN BLEND*. Place the eggplant wedges, skin side down, in a 10x14 inch baking pan and bake for about 20 minutes, until browned. Remove baking pan from oven and set aside to cool. **Set oven temperature to 400 degrees.**

Prepare Filling & Sauce: In a large frying pan, sauté the filling ingredients, *except the pine nuts*, until the vegetables are lightly browned. Transfer to a bowl. Mix in the pine nuts and set aside. Place the sauce ingredients in the frying pan. Bring to a boil, reduce heat and simmer for 3 minutes (the sauce will be thin). Set aside.

Fill Boats and Bake: Working with the eggplant wedges in the baking pan, cut a 2 inch slit into each wedge along its length. Spread open along the slit to form a pocket. Do not cut through the skin. Press a heaping teaspoon of the filling into each pocket. Carefully spoon the tomato sauce over the top. Sprinkle with chopped parsley. Bake, uncovered, for 40 to 45 minutes until sauce has thickened and the eggplant is tender.

This is a great party dish because it can be prepared ahead and frozen without baking. Defrost before baking.

LUBIA BI ZEIT ❖
(Green Bean and Tomato Stew)
Makes 4 cups

3 Tbsp	olive oil
1 medium	onion, diced
1 clove	garlic, minced
1 1/2 Tbsp	*SPICE BAZAAR ATHENIAN GARDEN SPICE*
1 15 oz can	diced tomatoes
1 lb	green beans, fresh or frozen
1 cup	water

Place oil, onion, garlic and *ATHENIAN GARDEN SPICE* in a medium saucepan and sauté over moderately high heat until onion is lightly browned. Add tomatoes, green beans and water and bring to a boil. Reduce heat and simmer, covered, for 20 to 30 minutes until beans are tender and sauce is thick. If you are using fresh green beans, cook 10 to 15 minutes longer, adding more water if necessary. Serve over Syrian Rice (page 40).

FALAFEL ❖
(Fried Chick Pea Patties)
Makes 25-35 patties or balls

Throughout the Middle East, you will see street vendors with oversized woks frying Falafel and making sandwiches for hungry shoppers. In the United States, Falafel has become popular as a tasty, healthy alternative to fast food burgers.

2/3 cup	dry garbanzo beans, or dry peeled fava beans*, rinsed
1/4 cup	chopped parsley
1/2 cup	chopped onion
1/2 cup	plain bread crumbs
2 Tbsp	*SPICE BAZAAR JERICHO FALAFEL SPICE*
	oil for frying

Soak beans several hours or overnight. Drain and place in a food processor with the remaining ingredients. Process until fine, almost a paste. Shape into small patties or balls, using a level tablespoon of mix for each Falafel. If the mixture falls apart too easily, add a few more bread crumbs and perhaps a little water. Deep-fry a few at a time in a small pan with at least 2 inches of hot oil. When browned, remove and drain on paper towels.

To Serve: Place 5 or 6 patties in a pita with lettuce, sliced onion and tomato. Top with Tahini Sauce (page 57). Falafel balls are also popular as an appetizer for parties, with Tahini Sauce for dipping.

Variation: For those who do not wish to fry, try the following oven-baked method. The Falafel will not be as crispy but will be delicious, nonetheless. Flatten balls to 1/4 inch thick. Place on a parchment or foil-lined tray that has been lightly brushed with oil. Brush tops of Falafel with a little more oil. Bake in a preheated 400 degree oven for 20 minutes until lightly browned.

NOTE: Uncooked Falafel balls or patties freeze very well. It is not necessary to defrost before frying; just be sure the oil is hot.

*See Glossary of Ingredients page 165.

TAHINI SAUCE ✤
Makes 1 cup

1/2 cup	sesame tahini paste*
2 tsp	*SPICE BAZAAR SESAME TAHINI SAUCE AND DIP SPICE*
1/2 cup	water

Place sesame tahini paste, *SESAME TAHINI SAUCE AND DIP SPICE* and water in a small bowl and stir until smooth. Add more water as needed to obtain desired consistency. For a tangier flavor, add a little fresh lemon juice.

Tahini Sauce is also popular as a dip for fresh vegetables, crackers and pita wedges. Try Baked Fish with Tahini Sauce (page 88) and Kifta Baked with Tahini Sauce (page 101).

*See Glossary of Ingredients page 167.

DAL ✤
(Indian Lentils)
Makes 2 cups

Dal is served as a traditional accompaniment to Indian meals or may be served over rice as a main dish. Other kinds of lentils or beans may be substituted. Cooking times will vary, and water quantity should be adjusted as needed.

1 cup	brown lentils
3 cups	water
1 tsp	*SPICE BAZAAR GARAM MASALA INDIAN BLEND*
1 tsp	salt
2 thin	lemon slices
1 1/2 Tbsp	Clarified Butter (page 159) or olive oil
2 tsp	*SPICE BAZAAR GARAM MASALA INDIAN BLEND*

Rinse lentils. Place in a 2 quart pot with water, 1 tsp *GARAM MASALA INDIAN BLEND* and salt. Bring to a boil. Reduce heat and simmer, covered, for 30 to 40 minutes until lentils are tender. Add lemon slices and simmer 5 minutes more. If necessary, add a little water so the lentils will be soft and moist.

Heat Clarified Butter or oil in a small frying pan. Add 2 tsp *GARAM MASALA INDIAN BLEND* and stir over low heat until spices begin to darken. Stir the spiced butter or oil into cooked lentils.

MADRAS VEGETABLE STEW ❖

Makes 6 servings

This hearty vegetarian stew has many ingredients, but is very easy to prepare and cooks in less than 30 minutes.

1/4 cup	oil
1 medium	onion, diced
1 to 2 Tbsp	finely chopped fresh gingerroot
4 cloves	garlic, chopped
2 to 4	jalapeño peppers, seeded and chopped
1 Tbsp	*SPICE BAZAAR GARAM MASALA INDIAN BLEND*

1 cup	red lentils, rinsed
1 small	eggplant, cut into 1 inch cubes
1/2 lb	green beans, cut into 1 inch pieces
1 large	carrot, peeled and cut diagonally into 1/2 inch pieces
1 large	tomato, diced
1/4 cup	chopped cilantro
2 Tbsp	tamarind paste*
3 cups	water

Heat oil in a large saucepan. Add onion, gingerroot, garlic, jalapeños and *GARAM MASALA INDIAN BLEND*. Sauté over moderately high heat, until onions are golden brown. Add the remaining ingredients. Bring to a boil. Reduce heat and simmer, covered, for 20 to 25 minutes, stirring occasionally, until vegetables are tender and stew is thick. Add water as needed to keep the stew from sticking to the pot.

NOTE: Jalapeño peppers are very hot. Wash hands and utensils thoroughly after chopping. Rubber or plastic gloves may be used if hands are sensitive.

*See Glossary of Ingredients page 167.

NEW DELHI EGGPLANT STEW ✤
Makes 4 to 6 servings

2 medium	eggplants
2 medium	onions, sliced 1/4 inch thick
2 cloves	garlic, minced
4 Tbsp	oil, divided
1 1/2 tsp	*SPICE BAZAAR GARAM MASALA INDIAN BLEND*
2 medium	tomatoes, diced
1 medium	red pepper, diced
1 cup	water

Slice eggplants into 1/4 inch rounds and then into 1/4 inch strips. Place in a colander and sprinkle generously with salt. Set aside for 15 minutes to draw out juices.

Heat 2 Tbsp oil in a large, non-stick frying pan. Add onions, garlic and *GARAM MASALA INDIAN BLEND* and sauté until onions are lightly browned. Transfer to a large saucepan.

Rinse eggplant in cold water, drain and gently squeeze dry with paper towels. Heat 2 more Tbsp oil in the frying pan. Add eggplant and sauté over moderately high heat until lightly browned. Transfer to the saucepan and add tomatoes, red pepper and water. Simmer 20 minutes until soft and well cooked.

Serve over Basmati or Jasmine Rice (page 38).

MEATLESS MOUSSAKA ◆
(Greek Eggplant Casserole)
Makes 8 to 10 servings

This meatless version of the famous Moussaka is surprisingly satisfying. Follow the steps for preparation in the order given and it will go together smoothly and easily. As you complete each step of the preparation, take a minute to clean up the cooking utensils used and your final cleanup will be much easier.

Meatless Tomato Sauce:

2 Tbsp	olive oil
1 cup	diced onion
2 cloves	garlic, crushed

1 15 oz can	crushed tomatoes
1 cup	water
1/4 cup	red wine
1 cup	plain bread crumbs
1/2 cup	chopped parsley
1 1/2 Tbsp	SPICE BAZAAR GREEK SALAD DRESSING BLEND
1 Tbsp	SPICE BAZAAR ATHENIAN GARDEN SPICE

3 medium	zucchini, diced

Potatoes and Eggplant:

4 medium	potatoes, peeled and cut into 1/4 inch slices
2 medium	eggplants, cut into 1/2 inch round slices
1/4 cup	olive oil
	SPICE BAZAAR GREEK SALAD DRESSING BLEND

Cheese Sauce:

1/3 cup	butter
1/3 cup	flour
1 tsp	SPICE BAZAAR RANDA'S SPICE
3 cups	milk
2	eggs
1 cup	grated mizethra* or Parmesan cheese, divided

Additional Ingredients for Assembly:

2 Tbsp	butter, melted
1/2 cup	plain bread crumbs
	SPICE BAZAAR GREEK SALAD DRESSING BLEND
	ground nutmeg

Preheat oven to broil. Spray a 10x14 inch baking pan with non-stick spray.

Meatless Tomato Sauce: Heat oil in a large saucepan. Add onion and garlic and sauté until lightly browned. Add the remaining tomato sauce ingredients, *except zucchini*, and simmer 10 minutes. If sauce becomes too thick more water may be added. It should be like thick spaghetti sauce. While sauce is cooking, blanch zucchini until tender-crisp. Drain and set aside. Or microwave for 2 to 3 minutes until tender-crisp. Stir into the sauce.

Potatoes and Eggplant: Place sliced potatoes in boiling water to cover and simmer until done, but still firm, about 5 to 7 minutes. Drain and set aside. Line a shallow baking pan with foil. Drizzle with olive oil. Place eggplant slices on pan and turn to coat both sides with oil. Sprinkle with GREEK SALAD DRESSING BLEND. Place under broiler for 5 minutes on each side, until browned. Set aside. **Immediately set oven temperature to 350 degrees.**

Cheese Sauce: Melt butter in a medium saucepan over medium heat. Add flour and RANDA'S SPICE, whisking briskly until thick and bubbly. Remove from heat and gradually whisk in the milk. Return to medium heat and bring to a boil, stirring constantly. Simmer 1 to 2 minutes, until sauce thickens. Remove from heat again. Place eggs in a small bowl and beat thoroughly. Slowly pour 1 cup sauce into eggs, beating continuously. Then pour egg mixture into remaining sauce, whisking continuously. Return to heat and cook just until it comes to a boil. Stir in half of the cheese, reserving the rest for later.

Assembly: Drizzle baking pan with 2 Tbsp melted butter. Spread with 1/2 cup bread crumbs. Sprinkle crumbs with GREEK SALAD DRESSING BLEND. Lay potato slices on top of crumbs. Spread tomato sauce on top of potatoes. Place eggplant slices over the sauce. Then pour cheese sauce on top. Sprinkle with reserved grated cheese and a little nutmeg. Bake in a 350 degree oven for 40 to 50 minutes, until cheese sauce is browned. Allow the Moussaka to set for 10 to 15 minutes before cutting into squares and serving.

Moussaka can be prepared ahead and refrigerated or frozen unbaked. If frozen, allow an extra 45 minutes to bake.

*See Glossary of Ingredients page 166.

MEATLESS PASTICCIO ◆
(Greek Macaroni Casserole)
Makes 8 to 10 servings

As with Moussaka, the secret to easy preparation is assembling all of the ingredients before beginning and completing the sections one at a time in the order given.

1 lb   Greek macaroni #1 or #2* (if these are not available, substitute ziti or mostaccioli pasta)

White Sauce:
3 Tbsp	butter
3 Tbsp	flour
2 cups	milk
2 tsp	*SPICE BAZAAR RANDA'S SPICE*

1 recipe   Meatless Tomato Sauce from Meatless Moussaka (page 60)

1 recipe   Cheese Sauce from Meatless Moussaka (page 60)

Preheat oven to 350 degrees. Spray a 10x14 inch baking pan with non-stick spray.

Cook macaroni according to package directions, taking care not to overcook. Drain, rinse in cold water and place in a large bowl. While macaroni is cooking, prepare the White Sauce.

White Sauce: In a medium saucepan, melt butter and whisk in flour and *RANDA'S SPICE*. Remove from heat and gradually whisk in milk. Return to heat and bring to a boil, stirring constantly. Simmer 1 minute. The sauce should be fairly thin. Pour over drained macaroni and gently mix in.

Assembly: Place half of the macaroni in the baking pan. Spread the tomato sauce over the macaroni. Place the rest of the macaroni over the tomato sauce. Spread the cheese sauce on top and sprinkle with reserved grated cheese. Bake for 40 to 50 minutes, until cheese sauce is browned. Let it set for 10 to 15 minutes before cutting into squares and serving.

Pasticcio can be made ahead and refrigerated or frozen unbaked. Allow 45 minutes extra baking time if frozen.

*See Glossary of Ingredients page 165.

SPINACH FETTUCCINE WITH
BÉCHAMEL SAUCE AND VEGETABLES ◆
Makes 4 servings

Our daughter, Deena, created this recipe for a quick-fix meal after a long day at work. While the fettuccine is cooking, she prepares the sauce and vegetables and has dinner on the table in 30 minutes.

6 oz	spinach fettuccine
1	carrot, peeled and cut into thin julienne strips
1 small	zucchini, cut into 1/2 inch pieces
1 cup	broccoli florets
2 whole	green onions, cut into 1/2 inch pieces
1/2 cup	sliced fresh mushrooms
1 Tbsp	*SPICE BAZAAR ATHENIAN GARDEN SPICE*
1 1/2 cups	Béchamel Sauce (page 159)

Prepare fettuccine according to package directions. When the fettuccine is almost al dente, add carrots, zucchini and broccoli to the boiling pasta water. Boil for 2 to 3 minutes. Drain pasta and vegetables thoroughly. Place in a bowl and add green onions, sliced mushrooms and *ATHENIAN GARDEN SPICE*. Mix in 1 cup Béchamel Sauce. Serve the remaining sauce on the side for those who prefer more.

SPANAKOPITA ♦
(Spinach and Cheese in Filo)
Makes 9x13 inch pan

White Sauce:

2 Tbsp	Butter
2 Tbsp	Flour
2 tsp	*SPICE BAZAAR RANDA'S SPICE*
1 cup	milk

Filling:

2 10 oz pkgs	frozen chopped spinach, defrosted
1/2 lb	feta cheese, crumbled (about 2 cups)
1/2 cup	small curd cottage cheese
1/2 cup	finely diced onion
1/4 cup	chopped parsley
2	eggs
2 Tbsp	lemon juice
1/4 tsp	nutmeg
4 tsp	*SPICE BAZAAR HELLENIC HERB BLEND*
1 lb	12x17" filo dough, defrosted
2/3 cup	Clarified Butter, melted (page 159)

Preheat oven to 350 degrees. Brush a 9x13 inch baking pan with Clarified Butter.

White Sauce: Melt butter in a small pan. Stir in the flour and *RANDA'S SPICE* and cook until smooth and bubbly. Gradually stir in the milk. Cook over medium heat, stirring constantly, until the mixture comes to a boil and thickens. Set aside to cool.

Filling: Squeeze excess water from spinach and place in a bowl. Add White Sauce and remaining filling ingredients. Mix well.

Assembly: Work with half of the stack of dough at a time, keeping the rest covered first with a piece of wax paper and then with a very slightly damp towel. Place two sheets of filo dough in the buttered baking pan with the filo extending up the sides of the pan. Brush generously with Clarified Butter. Place two more sheets in the pan and brush with butter again. Repeat with six more sheets, buttering between each two sheets. Spread the filling evenly over the dough. Turn the edges of the dough in to enclose the filling.

Cut the rest of the stack of filo to fit the pan. Lay the scraps on top of the filling and drizzle with butter. Next, lay 2 sheets of the cut filo on top of the filling and brush with butter. Repeat the layering and buttering procedure until all of the filo is used up. Pour any leftover butter on top. With a sharp knife, cut the top stack of filo into three rows lengthwise and 5 rows widthwise to make 15 squares. Bake for 40 to 50 minutes until golden brown. Let it cool 10 to 15 minutes. Cut through all layers and serve.

NOTE: See Spanakopita Triangles (page 4) for the appetizer version of this popular Greek dish.

MINI ZUCCHINI FRITTATAS ◆
Makes 4 to 5 servings

This Frittata variation makes a quick and easy brunch entrée. It also makes a great sandwich with sliced tomatoes and lettuce. For a light dinner, serve with salad and some steamed broccoli sprinkled with *SPICE BAZAAR ATHENIAN GARDEN SPICE*.

8	eggs
2 Tbsp	*SPICE BAZAAR EGYPTIAN LENTIL SOUP SPICE*
1 cup	flour
2 medium	zucchini, grated
1/2 cup	minced onion
4 Tbsp	butter, divided

In a medium bowl, whisk eggs and *EGYPTIAN LENTIL SOUP SPICE* until frothy. Gradually whisk in flour. Stir in zucchini and onion. Melt 2 Tbsp butter in a 12 inch non-stick frying pan. When butter is hot, spoon egg mixture into pan to form 4 or 5 hamburger-sized patties. Cover and cook over medium heat 3 to 4 minutes until bottom is browned and eggs are set. Uncover. Turn patties over and cook on second side for 1 minute until browned. Remove Frittatas to a serving platter and keep warm. Add 2 more Tbsp butter to pan and repeat cooking procedure to make 4 or 5 more Frittatas.

VEGETABLE SIDE DISHES

The following recipes are examples of simple vegetables given a new twist with different SPICE BAZAAR BLENDS. Substitute vegetables to suit your family's taste and try experimenting with different blends to go with your main dish.

HELLENIC CARROTS AND ZUCCHINI ❖
Makes 4 servings

1/2 lb	carrots, peeled and cut into julienne strips
2 medium	zucchini, cut into julienne strips
1 Tbsp	butter or oil
1 tsp	*SPICE BAZAAR HELLENIC HERB BLEND*

In a small saucepan, boil carrots in water to cover until half cooked, 3 to 4 minutes. Drain well. Heat butter or oil in a large shallow frying pan. Add carrots, zucchini and *HELLENIC HERB BLEND*. Sauté over high heat until carrots and zucchini are tender-crisp.

VEGETABLE KABOBS ❖
Makes 4 to 6 servings

1 each	zucchini, crooked neck and summer squash, cut into 1 inch pieces
1 each	green, red and yellow bell peppers, cut into 1 inch pieces
1 large	onion, cut into chunks
8	cherry tomatoes
8 large	mushrooms
1 cup	Greek Marinade (page 82)

Put all the vegetables in a bowl and pour the Greek Marinade over them. Or place all the ingredients in a gallon size zip-lock bag. Close and place on a plate. Marinate in the refrigerator several hours or overnight, turning occasionally. Alternate the different vegetables on skewers and grill over hot coals.

ORANGE-GLAZED BABY CARROTS ❧
Makes 4 servings

1 lb	baby carrots

Orange Glaze:

1 Tbsp	butter or oil
1 Tbsp	frozen orange juice concentrate
1 Tbsp	honey
1/2 tsp	ground cloves
2 tsp	SPICE BAZAAR ATHENIAN GARDEN SPICE

Cook carrots in boiling water until tender-crisp, about 10 minutes. Drain and set aside.

Orange Glaze: Melt butter in a large shallow frying pan. Add the remaining Orange Glaze ingredients and simmer 1 minute. Add carrots and cook over medium heat 1 minute, until carrots are glazed.

GARLICKY ENDIVE ❧
Makes 2 cups

2 large	bunches endive or collard greens
1/4 cup	extra virgin olive oil
1 1/2 to 2 tsp	SPICE BAZAAR JERUSALEM HUMMUS SPICE

Cut endive or collard greens into 2 inch pieces and rinse thoroughly. Drain and place in a large pot. It is not necessary to add water. Cover and cook over high heat until steam escapes from the pot. Reduce heat and simmer 10 to 15 minutes until greens are tender.

When the greens are done, drain into a colander and set aside until cool enough to handle. Squeeze out excess water and place in a medium bowl. Add olive oil and ***JERUSALEM HUMMUS SPICE*** and mix well.

Garlicky Endive can be served at room temperature, but the flavor improves if it is chilled. It is a flavorful addition to any meal, and is especially good with barbecued meats and chicken.

ZUCCHINI AND ONION SAUTÉ ✤
Makes 4 servings

This vegetable dish lends itself to almost any menu, with the added bonus of quick and easy preparation.

2 medium	zucchini, cut into 1/2 inch pieces
1 cup	sliced onion
2 Tbsp	olive oil
2 tsp	*SPICE BAZAAR ATHENIAN GARDEN SPICE*
1 medium	ripe tomato, diced

Place zucchini, onion and oil in a large, shallow frying pan. Sprinkle with *ATHENIAN GARDEN SPICE*. Sauté until vegetables are lightly browned. Add the diced tomato. Cover and simmer 2 to 3 minutes.

FRENCH CAULIFLOWER ◆
Makes 4 servings

1 medium	head cauliflower
1/2 medium	red pepper, sliced into 1/4 inch strips
1/3 cup	Herbed French Vinaigrette (page 26)
2 Tbsp	finely chopped parsley
2/3 cup	plain yogurt

Cut cauliflower into florets. Place florets, red pepper strips and 1 cup water in a medium saucepan. Steam until tender-crisp, 3 to 4 minutes. Drain in a colander and rinse under cold running water. In a medium bowl, blend together Herbed French Vinaigrette, parsley and yogurt. Add cauliflower and red pepper and turn gently to coat. Marinate 10 to 15 minutes before serving. Serve at room temperature, or refrigerate and serve as a cold salad.

POULTRY

SEAFOOD

◆ Denotes Vegetarian

OVEN-FRIED CHICKEN
Makes 4 to 6 servings

When our youngest daughter, Randa, was 10 years old, she wanted to make fried chicken. In order to simplify the job for her, I blended the spices in a shaker and let her have the run of the kitchen. This was my first spice blend. The following recipe is a healthy version of the old-fashioned fried chicken. It is so tasty that your family will not believe it was baked and not fried.

3 to 3 1/2 lb	skinless chicken pieces
2 1/2 Tbsp	SPICE BAZAAR RANDA'S SPICE, divided
1 1/2 tsp	SPICE BAZAAR ETHIOPIAN HOT SPICE (optional)
1/2 cup	flour
1/2 cup	plain bread crumbs
2	eggs
3 Tbsp	milk
1/3 cup	oil, divided

Preheat oven to 425 degrees. Line a shallow baking pan with parchment, or use foil and spray with non-stick spray. Drizzle the pan with half of the oil.

Rinse chicken and pat dry. Place in a bowl and sprinkle with 1 1/2 Tbsp *RANDA'S SPICE* and the *ETHIOPIAN HOT SPICE*. Turn to distribute the spice on the chicken pieces. Place the flour in a plastic bag. Place the bread crumbs and 1 Tbsp *RANDA'S SPICE* in another plastic bag. Shake to mix. Place the eggs and milk in a medium bowl and beat lightly.

To Coat Chicken: Shake 2 or 3 chicken pieces in the flour bag and place them on a platter. Repeat with the rest of the chicken. Next dip the chicken pieces in the egg mixture, one at a time, and place them back on the platter. Finally, shake the pieces in the bag of bread crumbs and place on the baking tray. DO NOT CROWD so they will brown well. Drizzle the rest of the oil on top. Bake for 30 minutes. Turn and continue baking for 10 to 15 minutes more until browned and finger lickin' good.

Variations: Boneless, skinless breasts, thighs or chicken tenders may be used. Increase baking temperature to 450 degrees. Bake for 20 to 30 minutes, turning after 15 minutes.

MAQLUBA
(Upside-down Eggplant and Chicken Casserole)
Makes 6 servings

Maqluba is a beautiful molded chicken dish that is prepared by cooking layers of eggplant, chicken and rice. It is served by inverting the cooked Maqluba onto a large round platter or tray.

Rice:

2 cups	calrose (pearl or medium grain) rice, rinsed well and drained
1/4 cup	dried minced onions
1/4 cup	chopped parsley
2 Tbsp	butter
4 cups	chicken broth
1/2 tsp	salt
1 1/2 tsp	*SPICE BAZAAR MIDDLE EASTERN BLEND*

Chicken:

2 lb	boneless skinless chicken breasts or thighs
	SPICE BAZAAR RANDA'S SPICE
2 Tbsp	butter

Eggplant:

1 medium	eggplant, cut into 1/2 inch round slices
3 Tbsp	olive oil
	SPICE BAZAAR RANDA'S SPICE
2 large	tomatoes, cut into 1/4 inch slices

Preheat oven to broil. Line a baking tray with foil. Spray a 6 quart, straight-sided pot with non-stick spray.

Prepare Rice: Place rice ingredients in a medium saucepan and bring to a boil. Reduce heat and simmer, covered, for 10 minutes until water is half-absorbed

Prepare Chicken: Rinse chicken and pat dry. Cut into 1 inch cubes and sprinkle with *RANDA'S SPICE*. Melt 2 Tbsp butter in a large, deep frying pan and sauté chicken until browned. Set aside.

Prepare Eggplant: Drizzle the baking tray with olive oil. Place the eggplant slices on the tray and turn to lightly coat both sides. Sprinkle with *RANDA'S SPICE*. Place under broiler for about 5 minutes on each side, until browned.

Assemble Maqluba: Lay the slices of tomato on the bottom of the 6 quart pot. Place the sautéed chicken over the tomatoes. Place the eggplant over the chicken. Spoon the rice on top of eggplant. Shake the pan gently so rice will fill the spaces between chicken and vegetables. Add 1/2 cup water. Cover pot and cook the Maqluba over high heat until steam escapes from lid, about 2 to 3 minutes. Immediately turn heat to low and cook for 15 minutes, until the rice is done. Turn off heat and let the pot sit for 15 to 30 minutes so the Maqluba will firm up before unmolding. When ready to serve, run a knife around edge of rice to loosen. Invert pot onto a large round serving platter or tray. Wait 10 minutes, then carefully lift pot off and serve.

Moroccan Onion and Raisin Chutney (page 12) and Tsatsiki (page 28) go especially well with Maqluba.

MOROCCAN BAKED CHICKEN WITH ONIONS
Makes 4 servings

3 to 3 1/2 lb	chicken pieces
2 large	onions, sliced
	SPICE BAZAAR MOROCCAN BLEND
1 cup	water

Preheat oven to 450 degrees. Spray a 9x13 inch baking pan with non-stick spray.

Rinse chicken and pat dry. Place in baking pan and sprinkle on both sides very generously with *MOROCCAN BLEND*. Top with sliced onions (lots of onions is what makes this dish so special). Cover tightly with foil and bake for 45 minutes until chicken is tender. Remove foil and continue baking for another 40 to 45 minutes, turning occasionally, until chicken is well browned and all the juices have evaporated. Do not rush this stage. It is the secret of this flavorful dish. When the juices have evaporated and the bottom of the pan is browned add 1 cup water. Replace foil and bake 5 to 10 minutes more to loosen all the drippings. Transfer chicken to a platter and spoon onions and pan juices on top.

Serve with Syrian Rice (page 40) and Fresh Tomato and Cucumber Salad (page 25).

CHICKEN OUZI
(Chicken and Rice Platter)
Makes 6 to 8 Servings

This exotic and flavorful dish is served in Jordan on special occasions and to honor special guests. It makes a beautiful presentation and is easy to prepare.

1	double recipe Basmati Rice (page 38)
4 lb	chicken pieces
	SPICE BAZAAR RANDA'S SPICE
	SPICE BAZAAR MIDDLE EASTERN BLEND
2 Tbsp	Clarified Butter (page 159)
1/4 cup	each pine nuts, blanched almonds and raw pistachios
1/4 cup	each white raisins and currants
1/2 lb	baby carrots
1/2 lb	frozen peas
4	eggs, hard boiled, peeled and cut in half

Preheat oven to 425 degrees. Spray a large shallow baking pan with non-stick spray.

Rinse chicken and pat dry. Place pieces in baking pan and sprinkle on both sides generously with *MIDDLE EASTERN BLEND* and then lightly with *RANDA'S SPICE*. Bake, uncovered, about 45 minutes, turning as needed until brown on both sides. Remove chicken and set aside. Add 1 cup water to pan and place over medium heat. Deglaze pan and pour drippings into a small bowl. Skim off fat. Set juices aside.

In a small frying pan, sauté pine nuts and almonds in Clarified Butter until golden brown. Stir in pistachios, white raisins and currants. Remove from heat and set aside. Steam carrots and peas separately in a small amount of water until tender crisp.

Arrange Platter: Spread rice on a large serving platter to within 2 inches of edge. Place chicken on top. Sprinkle nuts, white raisins and currants over chicken. Arrange carrots, peas and eggs around edge of platter. Pour chicken juices over all.

Tsatsiki (page 28) and a tossed salad with Lebanese Dressing (page 27) round out this beautiful meal.

JERICHO BAKED CHICKEN
Makes 4 servings

3 to 3 1/2 lb	chicken pieces
	SPICE BAZAAR RANDA'S SPICE
	SPICE BAZAAR JERICHO FALAFEL SPICE
1/3 cup	pine nuts or slivered almonds
2 Tbsp	Clarified Butter (page 159)
2 cups	sliced red onions
	parsley sprigs for garnish

Preheat oven to 425 degrees. Spray a large, shallow baking pan with non-stick spray.

Rinse chicken and pat dry. Place chicken pieces in baking pan and sprinkle lightly on both sides with *RANDA'S SPICE* and very generously with *JERICHO FALAFEL SPICE*. Bake uncovered 40 to 45 minutes until browned, turning once.

Meanwhile, in a medium frying pan sauté pine nuts in Clarified Butter over medium heat until golden brown. Remove nuts and set aside. Add onions to pan and sauté until they begin to brown slightly. Set aside.

When chicken is done, remove from oven and transfer to an oven-safe shallow casserole or platter. Spread onions on top and return to oven for 10 minutes. Sprinkle with pine nuts and garnish with sprigs of parsley.

Serve with Syrian Rice (page 40) and Tahini Salad (page 25).

MOROCCAN CHICKEN COUSCOUS
Makes 6 to 8 servings

1	double recipe Moroccan Couscous Pilaf (page 43)
3 lb	chicken pieces, skinned
1 Tbsp	*SPICE BAZAAR MOROCCAN BLEND*
3 Tbsp	Clarified Butter (page 159)
2 cups	water
1/2 lb	baby carrots
2 small	red or white potatoes, peeled and cut into 1 inch cubes
1 15 oz can	small fava beans* or garbanzo beans
2 small	turnips, cut into 1/2 inch cubes
1/2 lb	zucchini, cut into 1/2 inch cubes
1/2 lb	banana squash, peeled and cut into 1/2 inch cubes
1/4 cup	chopped cilantro
1/4 cup	chopped parsley
1/2 cup	dried apricots, cut in half
1/4 cup	white raisins
1/4 cup	currants
1/4 cup	pine nuts toasted
1/4 cup	whole blanched almonds, toasted

Rinse chicken and pat dry. Sprinkle with *MOROCCAN BLEND*. Melt Clarified Butter in a large deep frying pan. Place chicken in pan and brown on all sides. Add water and bring to a boil. Reduce heat and simmer, covered, until chicken is done, 35 to 40 minutes. Remove chicken and set aside, leaving juices in pan.

Place baby carrots and potatoes in the pan with the juices and add a little more water if needed to cover. Cook about 10 minutes, until carrots and potatoes are half cooked. Then add the rest of the vegetables (and a little more water if needed) and cook 5 to 10 minutes until the vegetables are almost done.

While vegetables are cooking, remove the chicken meat from the bones and set aside. When the vegetables are almost done, return the chicken to the pan with the apricots, raisins, currants, pine nuts and almonds. Again, add a little more water, if needed. Simmer for 5 minutes more. The secret of this recipe is to add small amounts of water at a time, as needed, so that the vegetables and chicken are always simmering in a rich, thick sauce.

To Serve: Spread Moroccan Couscous Pilaf on a large serving platter and top with the chicken and vegetables. Pour sauce over all.

*See Glossary of Ingredients page 165.

CASBAH CHICKEN WITH DRIED FRUIT AND NUTS
Makes 4 servings

The intriguing combination of flavors in this recipe will be the hit of your next dinner party.

1/4 cup	currants
1/4 cup	white raisins
10	dried apricots, cut in half
2 Tbsp	pine nuts
1/4 cup	blanched almonds
1/4 cup	Clarified Butter (page 159)
3 to 3 1/2 lb	chicken pieces
	SPICE BAZAAR MOROCCAN BLEND
1 cup	water
1 recipe	Moroccan Couscous Pilaf (page 43)

Place the currants, white raisins and apricots in a bowl and set aside.

In a large, deep frying pan, sauté pine nuts and almonds in Clarified Butter until golden brown. Remove nuts and transfer to the bowl with the dried fruit. Set aside.

Rinse chicken and pat dry. Sprinkle very generously on both sides with *MOROCCAN BLEND*.

Place chicken in frying pan and brown well on both sides. Add water. Cover and simmer 35 to 40 minutes, turning occasionally and adding more water, a little at a time as needed, until chicken is almost done. Stir in the dried fruit. Check to see that there is still some juice in the pan. If necessary, add a little more water again so you will have a rich sauce to pour over the Couscous. Continue cooking until chicken is done. Stir in the nuts.

To Serve: Place prepared Moroccan Couscous Pilaf on a serving platter. Arrange chicken over the Couscous. Spoon fruit and nuts on top and pour juices over all.

ETHIOPIAN CHICKEN STEW
Makes 4 to 6 servings

This very easy one-dish meal is mildly hot. You can increase or decrease the heat by adjusting the amount of *ETHIOPIAN HOT SPICE*.

1 large	red onion, sliced
4 medium	carrots, peeled and cut into 1 inch pieces
2 cloves	garlic, minced
2 tsp	*SPICE BAZAAR ETHIOPIAN HOT SPICE*
3 Tbsp	Clarified Butter (page 159)
2 15 oz cans	diced tomatoes
1 cup	water
1/4 cup	dry red wine
1 tsp	salt
3 to 3 1/2 lb	chicken pieces, skinned
4 medium	white rose or red potatoes, scrubbed and quartered
1/4 cup	chopped cilantro

Rinse chicken and set aside. In a large, deep frying pan, sauté red onion, carrots, garlic and *ETHIOPIAN HOT SPICE* in Clarified Butter until onion is translucent. Add diced tomatoes, water, wine and salt. Bring to a boil and simmer for 1 to 2 minutes. Add chicken, potatoes and cilantro. Bring to a boil. Reduce heat and simmer, covered, for 45 minutes, until chicken and vegetables are tender, turning chicken pieces occasionally. Add water as needed to keep it from drying out.

Serve with Ethiopian Berber Sauce (page 12) and a platter of fresh vegetables with Creamy Garlic Dressing.

CHICKEN IN TANDOORI ALMOND SAUCE
Makes 4 servings

3 to 3 1/2 lb	chicken pieces
1 cup	plain yogurt
1/4 cup	sour cream
1/2 cup	blanched almonds
1 medium	onion, diced
3 cloves	garlic, chopped
1/2 to 1 Tbsp	finely chopped fresh gingerroot
1 to 2	fresh jalapeño peppers, seeded
2 tsp	*SPICE BAZAAR TANDOORI BOMBAY BLEND*
1/4 cup	water
1/4 cup	oil, divided
	Paprika and chopped parsley for garnish
1 recipe	Basmati Rice (page 38) or Benares Pilao (page 41)

Rinse chicken and pat dry. Set aside. In a bowl, mix together yogurt and sour cream. Set aside. Place almonds, onion, garlic, gingerroot, jalapeño peppers, *TANDOORI BOMBAY BLEND* and water in a food processor or blender and process or blend until almost smooth.

Heat 2 Tbsp oil in a large deep frying pan. Add the processed almond mixture. Stir and fry for 5 minutes until lightly browned. Stir the almond mixture into the bowl with the yogurt and sour cream. Set aside.

Place 2 Tbsp more oil in frying pan and brown chicken on both sides. Pour Tandoori Almond Sauce over chicken. Bring to a gentle boil. Reduce heat and simmer, covered, for 35 to 45 minutes, until chicken is tender.

Transfer chicken to a serving platter and spoon some sauce on top. Sprinkle with paprika and chopped parsley. Serve the rest of the sauce in a gravy boat to pour over Basmati Rice or Benares Pilao.

CHICKEN GYROS
Makes 4 sandwiches

1 lb	boneless, skinless chicken breasts or thighs
1 Tbsp	*SPICE BAZAAR HELLENIC HERB BLEND*
1/2 tsp	salt
3 Tbsp	Clarified Butter (page 159) or olive oil
1 large	onion, sliced 1/4 inch thick
2 cups	shredded lettuce
1	tomato, sliced
1/2	red onion sliced
1 cup	Yogurt-Sour Cream Dressing (page 14)
4	pitas

Rinse chicken and pat dry. Cut into strips and sprinkle with *HELLENIC HERB BLEND* and salt. Set aside. Heat butter or oil in a large shallow frying pan. Add onions and sauté until translucent. Add chicken and sauté over moderately high heat about 5 minutes, until chicken is cooked and lightly browned. Do not overcook, as chicken will become dry. Serve in pita bread with lettuce, tomato, onion and Yogurt-Sour Cream Dressing.

For your next casual get-together, prepare all the ingredients for Chicken Gyros sandwiches and let your guests assemble their own. Add a Greek Salad (page 29) and some Hummus Dip (page 10) and relax as your guests enjoy the feast.

CHICKEN SOUVLAKI
(Greek Chicken Shish-kabob)
Makes 6 servings

2 lb	boneless skinless chicken breast
6	cherry tomatoes
6	mushrooms
1/2	green bell pepper, cut into 6 pieces
1/2	red bell pepper, cut into 6 pieces
1/2	yellow bell pepper, cut into 6 pieces
1 small	zucchini, cut into 6 pieces
1 recipe	Greek Marinade (page 82)

Rinse chicken breasts and pat dry. Cut into 1 inch cubes. Place in a bowl with half of the Greek Marinade and turn to coat. Cover and refrigerate 2 to 3 hours or overnight.

Place vegetables in a bowl with the rest of the marinade and refrigerate 2 to 3 hours or overnight.

Place the chicken on skewers, alternating pieces with the marinated vegetables. Grill over hot coals.

NOTE: Souvlaki may also be prepared with leg of lamb, pork tenderloin or top sirloin (page 99).

GREEK BAKED CHICKEN
Makes 4 servings

3 to 3 1/2 lb   chicken pieces
1 recipe   Greek Marinade (page 82)
            paprika

Rinse chicken and pat dry. Place in a bowl with marinade and turn to coat. Refrigerate 1 to 2 hours or overnight.

Preheat oven to 450 degrees. Spray a 9x13 inch baking pan with non-stick spray.

Place chicken, skin side down, in baking pan. Bake uncovered for 20 minutes. Turn and sprinkle with paprika. Continue baking 20 to 25 minutes more, until tender and browned. Transfer chicken to a platter. Add 1 cup water to pan and place over medium heat. Deglaze pan and pour drippings into a small bowl. Skim off fat. Pour drippings over the chicken.

Serve with Rice Pilaf (page 42) and a Greek Salad (page 29).

GREEK MARINADE ❖
Makes 1 cup

1/2 cup	olive oil
1/2 cup	lemon juice
2 cloves	garlic, crushed
2 Tbsp	*SPICE BAZAAR GREEK SALAD DRESSING BLEND*

Place all the ingredients in a small bowl and whisk until thick.

Use as a marinade for chicken, meats, fish or vegetables.

TANDOORI CHICKEN
Makes 4 servings

3 to 3 1/2 lb	chicken pieces
1 cup	plain yogurt
2 Tbsp	*SPICE BAZAAR TANDOORI BOMBAY BLEND*
	paprika (for the Oven-baked variation)

Rinse chicken and pat dry. Cut two or three deep gashes in each chicken piece. Mix yogurt and *TANDOORI BOMBAY BLEND* in a large bowl. Add chicken and turn to coat. Refrigerate, covered, for 2 to 3 hours or overnight. Grill over hot coals until chicken is tender and juices run clear.

To Oven-bake: Place the marinated chicken, skin side down, in a 9x13 inch baking pan. Pour extra marinade over the top. Sprinkle with paprika and bake at 400 degrees until browned 30 to 40 minutes. Turn and sprinkle again with paprika and continue baking until browned and chicken is tender, 10 to 15 minutes more.

For Tandoori Chicken Kabobs: Cut boneless, skinless chicken breasts into 1 inch cubes. Prepare the yogurt marinade and marinate the chicken as above. Place on skewers and grill.

Serve with Benares Pilao (page 41) and Spinach Salad with Lebanese Dressing (page 27).

ANGIE'S FILO-WRAPPED CHICKEN BREASTS
Makes 8 servings

This is an elegant chicken dish which our family created for our oldest daughter Angela's wedding. It was an immediate success and has been served at many weddings since. Serve it with Rice Pilaf (page 42), Hellenic Carrots and Zucchini (page 66) and a tossed salad with Herbed French Vinaigrette (page 26).

1/2 cup	melted Clarified Butter (page 159), divided
8	boneless chicken breasts, 4 to 5 oz each
4 oz	smoked ham (4 slices, cut in half)
4 oz	provolone or Monterey Jack cheese (cut into 8 slices)
1 6 oz jar	marinated artichoke hearts, cut in half
	SPICE BAZAAR RANDA'S SPICE
3/4 lb	12x17" filo dough, defrosted (see Handling Filo Dough, page 161)

Preheat oven to 400 degrees. Line a shallow baking pan with parchment, or use foil and spray with non-stick spray. Drizzle with 2 Tbsp Clarified Butter.

Rinse chicken breasts and pat dry. Remove some, but not all, of the skin. Sprinkle lightly on each side with *RANDA'S SPICE*. Pound lightly with a mallet to flatten to 1/2 inch thick. Place 1 piece of ham, 1 slice of cheese and 1 piece of artichoke heart on one side of each breast and fold over. Tuck in any narrow end pieces of the breast so you have a neat package.

Lay a sheet of filo on the table with the narrow side toward you. Brush lightly with Clarified Butter. Lay a second sheet on top and brush lightly with butter again. Place the stuffed chicken breast on the filo, about 3 inches from the edge nearest you. Fold the end over and the sides in. Brush the folded edges with Clarified Butter. Fold over to the end to make a square shape. Place the wrapped breast, seam side down, on the baking tray. Repeat with the rest of the breasts. Avoid crowding so they will brown well. Brush with the remaining Clarified Butter. Bake about 45 minutes, brushing with butter from the bottom of the pan once or twice, until golden brown.

HINT: Unbaked filo-wrapped breasts freeze well. Place prepared breasts on baking sheet. Wrap well with plastic wrap and place in freezer. Defrost overnight in the refrigerator before baking.

MONA'S FILO-WRAPPED CHICKEN WITH SPINACH AND RICOTTA FILLING

Makes 1 roll, 4 to 5 servings

This recipe was developed for our daughter Mona's wedding. Just like the Filo-wrapped Chicken Breast recipe for her sister, Angie, it was an immediate success and has become a popular wedding entrée. It is also delicious when prepared with turkey breast or firm fish filets in place of the chicken breasts.

1/2 cup	melted Clarified Butter (page 159), divided

Filling:

1 10 oz pkg	frozen chopped spinach, defrosted
1	egg, lightly beaten
1/4 cup	plain bread crumbs
1/4 cup	diced onion
1/2 cup	ricotta cheese
1 Tbsp	lemon juice
1 Tbsp	Clarified Butter (page 159)
1 tsp	SPICE BAZAAR RANDA'S SPICE
1 tsp	SPICE BAZAAR HERBES DE FRANCE

Chicken Breasts and Filo:

1 1/2 lb	boneless, skinless turkey or chicken breast
	SPICE BAZAAR RANDA'S SPICE
1/2 lb	12x17" filo dough, defrosted (see Handling Filo Dough, page 161)

Preheat oven to 350 degrees. Line a shallow baking pan with parchment or foil and brush with Clarified Butter.

Squeeze excess water from spinach and place in a medium bowl. Mix in remaining filling ingredients. Set aside.

Rinse chicken breasts and pat dry. Sprinkle on both sides with *RANDA'S SPICE*. Lay the breasts between two layers of plastic wrap and pound lightly with a mallet or the flat side of a large knife blade, so most of the breasts are of even thickness. Set aside.

Place two sheets of filo on the table with the wide edge facing you. Brush lightly with Clarified Butter. Place 2 more sheets on top and brush lightly with butter again. Arrange breasts on the filo in a rectangular shape, leaving approximately a 2 inch border of filo all around. Spread the filling over the breast. Fold filo ends in and roll up. Set the roll aside. Place two sheets of filo on the table again and butter lightly. Place two more sheets on top and brush with butter. Repeat 2 more times (8 sheets total in the stack). Place the chicken roll in the center of this stack of dough. Fold ends in and roll up again. Place in the baking pan, seam side down. Brush with the rest of the Clarified Butter.

Bake for 45 to 55 minutes, until nicely browned, basting once or twice with butter from the bottom of the pan. Allow to cool 10 minutes. Slice roll into 8 to 10 slices.

Serve with Rice Pilaf (page 42), tossed salad with Herbed French Vinaigrette (page 26) and Orange-glazed Baby Carrots (page 67).

NOTE: Mona's Filo-wrapped Chicken Roll freezes well, unbaked. Defrost in the refrigerator overnight before baking.

TURKEY CUTLETS WITH ORANGE HERB SAUCE
Makes 4 servings

This elegant dish is surprisingly quick and easy to prepare. Add Moroccan Couscous Pilaf (page 43) and Spinach Salad with Lebanese Dressing (page 27) for a lovely and relaxing evening.

1 lb	turkey breast cutlets or tenders
	salt and pepper
	flour for coating
2 Tbsp	oil

Sauce:

1/2 cup	orange juice
1/4 cup	white wine
3/4 cup	chicken broth
1/2 tsp	*SPICE BAZAAR HERBES DE FRANCE*
2 Tbsp	cornstarch

Rinse turkey and pat dry. Pound with a mallet to 1/4 inch thick. Sprinkle lightly with salt and pepper and coat with flour. Heat oil in a medium frying pan. Add turkey cutlets and cook over moderately high heat until lightly browned (2 to 3 minutes). Turn and brown on second side (2 to 3 minutes). Be careful not to overcook! Remove cutlets and place on a serving platter.

Blend sauce ingredients in a bowl and add to the frying pan. Bring to a boil, stirring constantly. Reduce heat and simmer 1 to 2 minutes, until thick. Pour half of the sauce over the cutlets. Serve the rest in a gravy boat for those who prefer more sauce.

GREEK FRIED FISH
WITH AVGOLEMONO SAUCE ◆
Makes 3 to 4 servings

1 lb	fish filets (cod, perch, etc.), cut into 3 or 4 servings
	SPICE BAZAAR RANDA'S SPICE
	SPICE BAZAAR HELLENIC HERB BLEND
1/2 cup	flour
1/4 cup	salad oil
1 recipe	Avgolemono Sauce prepared with vegetable broth (page 21)
2 Tbsp	chopped parsley

Rinse filets and pat dry. Sprinkle on both sides with *RANDA'S SPICE* and *HELLENIC HERB BLEND* and dredge in flour. Heat oil in a shallow frying pan and add filets. Brown on both sides over medium heat. If filets are thick, reduce heat a little so they will cook through. When the fish has browned and flakes when pierced with a fork, transfer to a serving platter. Pour Avgolemono Sauce on top and sprinkle with chopped parsley.

Serve with Hellenic Carrots and Zucchini (page 66) and Greek Home-baked Potatoes (page 46).

LEBANESE FISH FILETS ◆
Makes 3 to 4 servings

1 lb	codfish filets
	SPICE BAZAAR LEBANESE KIFTA SPICE
1/2 cup	flour
1/4 cup	olive oil
	chopped parsley and lemon wedges for garnish

Follow the cooking procedure in the Greek Fried Fish recipe (above). When fish is done, transfer to a serving platter and sprinkle with parsley. Surround with lemon wedges.

Serve with Lebanese Hash Browns (page 46) and Tahini Salad (page 25).

BAKED FISH WITH TAHINI SAUCE ◆
Makes 6 servings

2 lb   firm fish (halibut, cod or perch)
1 recipe   Tahini Sauce (page 57)
         chopped parsley and lemon wedges for garnish

Preheat oven to 350 degrees. Line a 9x13 inch baking pan with foil and spray with non-stick spray.

Place fish in baking pan and bake for 20 to 30 minutes, until it almost flakes when pierced with a fork. Prepare Tahini Sauce using 2 to 3 Tbsp more water to make a thin sauce. Pour Tahini Sauce over the fish. Set the oven to broil and return the tray to the oven. Broil until the sauce is thick and bubbly and lightly browned on top.

Transfer fish to a platter and sprinkle with chopped parsley. Surround with lemon wedges. Serve with Jasmine Rice (page 38), Fresh Tomato and Cucumber Salad (page 25) and steamed broccoli sprinkled with *Spice Bazaar Shafik's Red Lentil Soup Spice*.

SWORDFISH KABOBS ◆
Makes 4 servings

1 to 1 1/4 lbs   swordfish or halibut filets
1/2 cup   plain yogurt
2 tsp   *Spice Bazaar Garam Masala Indian Blend*
1 tsp   salt

Rinse fish and pat dry. Cut into 1 inch cubes. Blend yogurt, *Garam Masala Indian Blend* and salt in a medium bowl. Add fish and turn to coat. Marinate 1 to 2 hours or overnight. Place on skewers and grill over hot coals until fish is cooked through, about 15 minutes. Do not overcook or fish will become dry.

Variation: Leave fish filets whole. Marinate and bake in a preheated 400 degree oven for 20 to 25 minutes, until fish flakes when pierced with a fork.

Serve with Garlicky Endive (page 67), Bulgur Pilaf (page 42) and Tahini Salad (page 25).

CODFISH IN ETHIOPIAN TOMATO SAUCE ◆

Makes 3 to 4 servings

3 Tbsp	olive oil
1 medium	onion, diced
1 clove	garlic, minced
1 tsp	*SPICE BAZAAR ETHIOPIAN HOT SPICE*
1 8 oz can	tomato sauce
1 cup	water
1 Tbsp	vinegar
1/2 tsp	sugar
	salt to taste
1 lb	codfish or red snapper filets

Heat oil in a large deep frying pan. Add onion, garlic and *ETHIOPIAN HOT SPICE* and sauté over medium heat, until onion is lightly browned. Add the remaining ingredients, *except the fish filets*, and simmer for 2 to 3 minutes. Place fish filets in pan and spoon sauce over them. Cover and simmer for 10 to 15 minutes, until fish flakes when pierced with a fork.

Serve with Jasmine Rice (page 38), Ethiopian Berbere Sauce (page 12) and Zucchini and Onion Sauté (page 68). A platter of fresh vegetables rounds out this quick and easy dinner.

ETHIOPIAN EGGPLANT AND SHRIMP ◆

Makes 4 to 6 servings

1 recipe	Ethiopian Eggplant Relish (page 13)
1 lb	cooked shrimp (medium to large size is best)

Prepare Ethiopian Eggplant Relish, adding 1/4 to 1/2 cup water if it is very thick. Stir in the shrimp and heat through. Serve over Moroccan Couscous Pilaf (page 43) or Syrian Rice (page 40).

MASALA TROUT WITH NUTS AND CURRANTS ◆
Makes 4 servings

4	trout, 10 to 12 oz, head removed and boned (ask butcher to do this for you)
1/4 cup	pine nuts or slivered almonds
1/4 cup	olive oil

Filling:

1 cup	finely diced onion
2 tsp	SPICE BAZAAR GARAM MASALA INDIAN BLEND
1/3 cup	finely chopped walnuts
1 cup	plain bread crumbs
1/3 cup	currants
2 Tbsp	lemon juice
1 tsp	salt

chopped parsley and lemon wedges for garnish

Preheat oven to 350 degrees. Line a 9x13 inch pan with parchment, or use foil and spray with non-stick spray.

In a medium frying pan, sauté pine nuts or slivered almonds in olive oil until golden brown. Remove nuts and set aside. Place onion and *GARAM MASALA INDIAN BLEND* in the frying pan and sauté until onion is translucent. Stir in the nuts and remaining filling ingredients.

Rinse trout and pat dry. Lay two of the trout flat, skin side down, in the baking pan. Spread the filling over the filets and lay the other two trout on top, skin side up.

Bake 25 to 30 minutes, until fish flakes when pierced with a fork. Transfer to a serving platter and garnish with chopped parsley and lemon wedges. Jasmine Rice (page 38) is a flavorful accompaniment to this recipe.

SHRIMP WITH FETA ◆
Makes 4 serving

2 Tbsp	olive oil
2 cups	sliced onion
2 cloves	garlic, minced
1 medium	green bell pepper, thinly sliced
1 Tbsp	*SPICE BAZAAR JERICHO FALAFEL SPICE*
2 medium	ripe tomatoes, diced
1 8 oz can	tomato sauce
1 lb	uncooked shrimp, peeled and deveined
1/3 lb	feta cheese, crumbled (about 1 1/4 cups)

Preheat broiler.

Heat oil in a large, deep frying pan. Add onion, garlic, green bell pepper and *JERICHO FALAFEL SPICE*. Sauté until onion is translucent. Add tomatoes and tomato sauce and cook 5 minutes, until tomatoes are soft. Add shrimp and cook just until shrimp begins to turn pink. Place in an ovenproof casserole. Sprinkle with feta. Place under broiler 2 to 3 minutes, until cheese melts and browns lightly.

Serve over Bulgur Pilaf (page 42) or Syrian Rice (page 40).

FILO-WRAPPED HALIBUT
WITH SPINACH AND RICOTTA FILLING ◆
Makes 1 roll, 4 to 5 servings

This variation of Mona's Filo-wrapped Chicken with Spinach and Ricotta Filling is an elegant and delicious main course. It is a welcome alternative to meat and chicken.

To prepare, use ingredients and follow instructions in the recipe for Mona's Filo-wrapped Chicken with Spinach and Ricotta Filling (page 84), substituting 1 1/2 lb halibut filets or other firm fish in place of the chicken.

SALMON TANDOORI ◆

Makes 6 servings

2 lb	salmon steaks
2 Tbsp	lemon juice
1/4 cup	olive oil
1 large	onion, diced
6 cloves	garlic, crushed
1 to 2 Tbsp	finely chopped gingerroot
1 Tbsp	***SPICE BAZAAR TANDOORI BOMBAY BLEND***
1 large	tomato, diced
1/4 cup	chopped cilantro

Sprinkle salmon steaks with lemon juice and set aside. Heat oil in a large shallow frying pan. Add onion, garlic, gingerroot and *TANDOORI BOMBAY BLEND.* Sauté over medium heat, until onion is lightly browned. Add diced tomato and simmer for 2 to 3 minutes. Place salmon steaks in pan and spoon sauce over them. Sprinkle with cilantro. Cover and simmer 10 to 15 minutes, until fish flakes easily when pierced with a fork.

Serve with a tossed salad with Creamy Garlic Dressing (page 14) and Fragrant Saffron Basmati Rice (page 40) sprinkled with toasted pine nuts and almonds.

MEATS

TENDER SLOW-ROASTED BEEF
Makes 6 to 8 servings

4 lb	sirloin tip roast
1 clove	garlic, crushed
1 Tbsp	olive oil
1 1/2 tsp	flour
1 Tbsp	*SPICE BAZAAR JORDANIAN ROAST LAMB SPICE*

Spray a baking pan with non-stick spray.

Make a paste of the garlic, olive oil, flour and *JORDANIAN ROAST LAMB SPICE*. Cut several slits in the roast and press half of the paste into the slits. Rub remaining paste over the entire roast. Place in baking pan, cover and refrigerate 2 to 3 hours or overnight. To bake, preheat oven to 450 degrees and bake uncovered for 20 minutes. Turn down temperature to 275 degrees and continue baking for 2 hours (30 minutes per lb). For accuracy, insert a meat thermometer in roast before roasting. Bake until desired stage is reached. Roast will continue to cook for a few minutes after removal from oven, so underbake slightly. Remove roast from pan and cover to keep warm while preparing gravy. Slice and serve with pan gravy.

Pan Gravy: Deglaze roasting pan by adding 1 1/2 cups water to the pan and scraping loose the drippings. Pour pan juices into bowl and skim off the fat. Place 1/4 cup flour in a small saucepan and gradually stir in pan juices, whisking continuously to keep smooth. Bring to a boil, reduce heat and simmer until thickened.

JORDANIAN ROAST LEG OF LAMB
Makes 6 to 8 servings

One 3 to 4 lb	boneless leg of lamb
OR	
One 6 to 8 lb	bone in leg of lamb
2 cloves	garlic, crushed
2 Tbsp	olive oil
1 Tbsp	flour
2 Tbsp	*SPICE BAZAAR JORDANIAN ROAST LAMB SPICE*

Make a paste of the garlic, olive oil, flour and *JORDANIAN ROAST LAMB SPICE*. Cut several slits in the leg of lamb and press half of the paste into the slits. Rub the remaining paste over the entire leg. Place in a roasting pan, cover tightly and refrigerate 2 to 3 hours or overnight.

Preheat oven to 450 degrees. Bake roast, uncovered, for 30 minutes. Reduce heat to 350 degrees. Cover roast and bake for 1 1/2 hours. Remove cover and turn roast over. Replace cover and continue baking for another hour or more, until the roast is well cooked and very tender. Transfer roast to a cutting board. Strain pan juices into a bowl and skim off the fat. Slice lamb and place on a serving platter. Pour some of the pan juices over the meat. Serve the rest for guests to add at the table. If not serving the lamb immediately, cover tightly with foil and place in oven at 150 degrees until ready to serve.

If desired, add onions, potatoes and other vegetables around the roast during the last hour.

NOTE: In the Middle East and Greece, lamb is always roasted until well done and very tender, almost falling off the bone. If you prefer your lamb medium rare or medium, use a roasting thermometer and bake, uncovered, until the desired stage is reached.

SHISH-KABOB
Makes 6 to 8 servings

1	leg of lamb, 6 to 8 lb or 3 lb boneless top sirloin of beef

2 tsp	*SPICE BAZAAR MIDDLE EASTERN BLEND*
1 Tbsp	wine vinegar
2 Tbsp	lemon juice
1/4 cup	olive oil
2 Tbsp	Worcestershire sauce
1/2 cup	chopped parsley
1 cup	finely minced onion
2 cloves	garlic, crushed

If using lamb, have your butcher cut off the shank end of the leg, bone the rest of the leg, and trim off all fat. Reserve the shank for Grecian Lamb Shanks with White Beans (page 115) or other recipes. If using top sirloin, trim away fat. Cut meat into 1 inch cubes. Place meat in a bowl and add the remaining ingredients. Turn to coat. Refrigerate several hours or overnight, turning occasionally. When ready to cook, skewer meat and grill over hot coals 10 to 20 minutes, until cooked to desired stage.

If desired, marinate chunks of onion, cherry tomatoes or other vegetables with the meat and skewer the vegetables alternately with the meat.

A traditional Shish-kabob dinner includes Syrian Rice (page 40), Hummus (page 10), Fresh Tomato and Cucumber Salad (page 25) and Tsatsiki (page 28).

GREEK ROAST LEG OF LAMB
Makes 6 to 8 servings

One 3 to 4 lb	boneless leg of lamb
OR	
One 6 to 8 lb	bone in leg of lamb
2 to 4 cloves	garlic
1/2 cup	olive oil
1/2 cup	lemon juice
1/4 cup	*SPICE BAZAAR GREEK SALAD DRESSING BLEND*

Cut slits into the leg of lamb and press slivers of garlic into the slits. Whisk together the olive oil, lemon juice and *GREEK SALAD DRESSING BLEND* and rub over the leg. Place in a roasting pan, cover tightly and refrigerate 2 to 3 hours or overnight.

Preheat oven to 450 degrees. Bake roast, uncovered, for 30 minutes. Reduce heat to 350 degrees. Cover roast and bake for 1 1/2 hours. Remove cover and turn roast over. Replace cover and continue baking for another hour or more, until the roast is well cooked and very tender. Transfer roast to a cutting board. Strain pan juices into a bowl and skim off the fat. Slice lamb and place on a serving platter. Pour some of the pan juices over the meat. Serve the rest for guests to add at the table. If not serving the lamb immediately, cover tightly with foil and place in oven at 150 degrees until ready to serve.

If desired, add onions, potatoes and other vegetables around the roast during the last hour.

NOTE: In the Middle East and Greece, lamb is always roasted until well done and very tender, almost falling off the bone. If you prefer your lamb medium rare or medium, use a roasting thermometer and bake, uncovered, until the desired stage is reached.

SOUVLAKI
(Greek-style Shish-kabob)
Makes 6 servings

2 lb	boneless leg of lamb, top sirloin or pork tenderloin
6	cherry tomatoes
6	mushrooms
1/2	green bell pepper, cut into 6 pieces
1/2	red bell pepper, cut into 6 pieces
1/2	yellow bell pepper, cut into 6 pieces
1 small	zucchini, cut into 6 pieces
1 medium	onion, cut into chunks
1 recipe	Greek Marinade (page 82)

Trim meat of all fat and cut into 1 inch cubes. Place in a bowl with half of the Greek Marinade and turn to coat. Cover and refrigerate 2 to 3 hours or overnight, turning occasionally.

Place vegetables in a bowl with the rest of the marinade and refrigerate 2 to 3 hours or overnight.

Place the meat on skewers, alternating pieces with the marinated vegetables. Grill over hot coals.

NOTE: Souvlaki may also be prepared with boneless, skinless chicken breasts (page 80).

KIFTA KABOBS
(Ground Meat Kabobs)
Makes 4 servings

1 lb	lean ground beef or lamb
1/2 cup	finely chopped parsley
1/2 cup	diced onion
1/2 cup	plain bread crumbs
2 1/2 tsp	*SPICE BAZAAR LEBANESE KIFTA SPICE*

Place all the ingredients in a bowl and mix thoroughly. Divide into 12 portions. Shape each portion into a sausage shape around a skewer, placing 2 or 3 kabobs on each skewer and grill over hot coals.

Serve in a pita pocket with chopped or sliced tomatoes and Tahini Sauce (page 57).

Variation: Divide into four portions and shape into patties. Grill or fry as you would hamburgers. Serve as above or in hamburger buns with lettuce, tomatoes and sliced onions.

KIFTA BAKED WITH POTATOES AND TOMATOES
Makes 4 to 6 servings

Ingredients from Kifta Kabobs recipe (above)

4 medium	potatoes, peeled and cut into 1/2 inch slices
4 medium	tomatoes, cut into 1/2 inch slices
2 Tbsp	butter, melted
	SPICE BAZAAR RANDA'S SPICE
	chopped parsley for garnish

Preheat oven to 350 degrees. Spray a 9x13 inch baking pan with non-stick spray.

Place ingredients from Kifta Kabobs recipe in a bowl and mix thoroughly. Press evenly into baking pan. Cook sliced potatoes in water to cover. Cover until almost done, 5 to 7 minutes. Drain and arrange potato and tomato slices alternately on top of meat. Drizzle with butter and sprinkle lightly with *RANDA'S SPICE*. Bake for 20 to 25 minutes, until meat is done and potatoes and tomatoes are lightly browned. Sprinkle with chopped parsley before serving.

KIFTA BAKED WITH TAHINI SAUCE
Makes 4 to 6 servings

Ingredients from Kifta Kabobs recipe (page 100)

1 recipe   Tahini Sauce (page 57)

Preheat oven to 350 degrees. Spray a 9x13 inch baking pan with non-stick spray.

Prepare the Tahini Sauce using 2 to 3 Tbsp more water to make a thin sauce. Set aside. Place ingredients from Kifta Kabobs recipe in a bowl and mix thoroughly. Press meat mixture evenly into baking pan. Bake for 20 minutes. Remove from oven and spread Tahini Sauce on top. Place under the broiler for 5 to 10 minutes, until lightly browned.

LUBIA BI LAHAM
(Green Bean and Lamb Stew)
Makes 6 cups

1 lb	boneless leg of lamb or lamb shoulder, cut into 1 inch cubes
1 Tbsp	olive oil
1 medium	onion, diced
1/2 tsp	salt
1/4 tsp	pepper
2 tsp	SPICE BAZAAR MIDDLE EASTERN BLEND
1 15 oz	can diced tomatoes
1 cup	water
1 lb	frozen green beans*

Trim lamb of excess fat and place in a large saucepan with olive oil, onion, salt, pepper and *MIDDLE EASTERN BLEND*. Sauté over moderately high heat, stirring frequently, until meat is browned. Add tomatoes and water.* Bring to a boil. Reduce heat and simmer, covered, for 20 minutes until meat is half cooked. Add green beans and return to a boil. Reduce heat and simmer, covered, 20 to 30 minutes more, until beans and meat are tender. Serve over Syrian Rice (page 40).

*If using fresh green beans, add them with the tomatoes and water.

KOOSA MAHSHI
(Stuffed Squash)
Makes 4 to 6 servings

The variety of squash used in the Middle East is a very light green and is sweeter tasting than our zucchini. However, small to medium zucchini may be substituted.

Stuffing Ingredients:

1/2 cup	parboiled rice (Uncle Ben's®)
1/2 cup	water
1/2 lb	lean ground beef or lamb
1/2 tsp	salt
1/4 tsp	pepper
1 tsp	*SPICE BAZAAR MIDDLE EASTERN BLEND*

Sauce Ingredients:

1 15 oz can	crushed tomatoes
1 tsp	salt
1/2 tsp	*SPICE BAZAAR MIDDLE EASTERN BLEND*
3 lb	small to medium zucchini

Place rice and water in a small saucepan. Bring to a boil. Reduce heat and simmer 5 to 7 minutes, until water is absorbed. Transfer to a medium bowl and let it cool slightly. Mix in meat, salt, pepper and *MIDDLE EASTERN BLEND*. Set aside.

Rinse zucchini well. If they are longer than 7 or 8 inches, cut them in half. With a vegetable reamer*, core out the inside of the zucchini, leaving a 1/8 inch to 1/4 inch shell. If you wish, you can set the cored out pulp aside to prepare the vegetable side dish below**. Use your fingers to push the filling into the zucchini, a little at a time, filling to within 1/2 inch of the opening. Do not pack the filling too tightly, or there will not be room for the rice to expand as it cooks. Lay the stuffed zucchini snugly side by side in a 4 to 6 quart pot, stacking in two layers as needed. Pour the can of crushed tomatoes on top. Sprinkle with the 1 tsp salt and the 1/2 tsp *MIDDLE EASTERN BLEND*. Add water to almost cover the zucchini and place a plate on top. Bring to a boil. Reduce heat and simmer, covered, for about 40 minutes or until the zucchini and rice are tender. Uncover and raise the heat to medium. Cook for 10 to 15 minutes to evaporate some of the liquid, making a nice thick sauce.

* A vegetable reamer is a long, narrow tool that is used to core out squash and other vegetables. The vegetables are then stuffed with various rice mixtures and cooked in sauces. Vegetable reamers are available at most Middle Eastern grocery stores.

** For a delicious vegetable side dish, sprinkle the zucchini pulp with *RANDA'S SPICE* and *MIDDLE EASTERN BLEND* and sauté it with diced onions and olive oil. If you have any of the meat and rice filling mixture left, add it to the pan after the pulp is cooked. Steam it for about 10 minutes until the rice is tender.

TESBINA'S FAVORITE
(Ground Meat with Tomatoes and Peas)
Makes 4 servings

This recipe was my mother's quick-fix meal when she was late with dinner and had a lot of hungry children waiting.

1 lb	lean ground beef or lamb
1/2 cup	diced onion
1 clove	garlic, minced
1/4 cup	chopped parsley
1 15 oz can	crushed tomatoes
1 lb	frozen peas
2 tsp	*SPICE BAZAAR DAMASCUS KIBBIE SPICE*
2 cups	water

Sauté ground meat, onion and garlic in a deep frying pan until browned. Add the remaining ingredients and bring to a boil. Reduce heat and simmer, covered, for 20 minutes, until thick.

Meanwhile, prepare Syrian Rice (page 40) and a tossed salad with Syrian Salad Dressing (page 24). Dinner will be on the table in 35 to 40 minutes.

SHEIKH EL MAHSHI
(Stuffed Eggplant Boats)
Makes 8 to 10 servings

The Arabic name of this dish translates to "The Sheik of Stuffed Dishes". It offers an impressive presentation and is especially delicious served over Syrian Rice (page 40).

2 large	eggplants
1/4 cup	Clarified Butter, melted (page 159)
	SPICE BAZAAR RANDA'S SPICE

Filling:

3/4 lb	lean ground beef or lamb
1 1/2 cups	diced onion
1 1/2 Tbsp	SPICE BAZAAR JORDANIAN ROAST LAMB SPICE
3 Tbsp	pine nuts or slivered almonds, toasted

Sauce:

2 15 oz cans	diced tomatoes
1 1/2 cups	water
1 Tbsp	SPICE BAZAAR JORDANIAN ROAST LAMB SPICE
3 Tbsp	chopped parsley

Preheat oven to 450 degrees.

Cut stems off the eggplants. Cut them in half lengthwise and then in half again across the middle. Cut each quarter into 2 or 3 wedges. Brush the cut surfaces with Clarified Butter and sprinkle with *RANDA'S SPICE*. Place the eggplant wedges, skin side down, in a 10x14 inch baking pan and bake for about 20 minutes, until browned. Remove baking pan from oven and set aside to cool. **Reduce oven temperature to 400 degrees.**

In a large frying pan, sauté the ground meat, diced onion and 1 1/2 Tbsp *JORDANIAN ROAST LAMB SPICE* over moderately high heat until browned. Transfer to a bowl. Mix in the pine nuts and set aside. Place the sauce ingredients in the frying pan. Bring to a boil, reduce heat and simmer for 3 minutes (the sauce will be thin). Set aside.

Working with the eggplant wedges in the baking pan, cut a 2 inch slit into each wedge along its length. Spread open along the slit to form a pocket. Do not cut through the skin. Press a heaping teaspoon of the filling into each pocket. Carefully spoon the tomato sauce over the top. Sprinkle with chopped parsley. Bake, uncovered, for 40 to 45 minutes until sauce has thickened and the eggplant is tender.

This is a great party dish because it can be prepared ahead and frozen without baking. Defrost before baking.

KIBBIE
(Ground Meat with Bulgur, Onions and Pine Nuts)
Makes a 9x13 inch pan or 25 to 30 Stuffed Kibbie Balls

Serve Baked Kibbie with Syrian Rice (page 40), Stuffed Grape Leaves (page 106), Tsatsiki (page 28) and a salad for a traditional Arabic "company's coming" meal.

Filling:

1 lb	lean ground beef or lamb
1 cup	diced onion
1/4 cup	pine nuts or slivered almonds, toasted
2 tsp	SPICE BAZAAR DAMASCUS KIBBIE SPICE

Kibbie Mixture:

2 lb	lean ground beef or lamb
2 cups	fine bulgur (#1)*
1 1/2 cups	water
2 cups	finely minced onion
2 1/2 Tbsp	SPICE BAZAAR DAMASCUS KIBBIE SPICE

Preheat oven to 350 degrees.

Filling: In a large frying pan, sauté filling meat and onion over moderately high heat until lightly browned. Drain off excess fat. Mix in pine nuts and *DAMASCUS KIBBIE SPICE*. Set aside.

Kibbie Mixture: Place kibbie mixture ingredients in a bowl and knead until thoroughly mixed. Or place the ingredients in the bowl of an electric mixer and mix until thoroughly blended. Mixture will be soft and will stiffen up as you proceed with assembly.

To Prepare the Kibbie in a Tray: Press half of the Kibbie mixture evenly in the bottom of a 9x13 inch baking pan. Spread the filling evenly over the layer of Kibbie. Form patties with the rest of the Kibbie mixture and lay them side-by-side on top of filling. Use bits of the mixture to fill in empty spaces. Smooth over entire pan with wet hands. Cut into 2 inch squares and then cut diagonally to form triangles. Bake for 40 to 45 minutes until lightly browned.

To Prepare Stuffed Kibbie Balls: These are popularly known as footballs because of their shape. Make balls using 2 Tbsp Kibbie mixture. Press a large indentation in the center. Fill with 1 Tbsp Kibbie filling. Close up and form into a football shape. Spray a baking pan with non-stick spray. Place the Kibbie Balls on tray and bake 35 to 40 minutes, until browned, turning occasionally.

To prepare Kibbie Ball Appetizers see page 6.

*See Glossary of Ingredients page 165.

DOLMADES
(Stuffed Grape Leaves)
Makes 40 to 50 Dolmades

3/4 cup	parboiled rice (Uncle Ben's®)
3/4 cup	water
3/4 lb	lean ground beef or lamb
1/2 tsp	salt
1/2 tsp	pepper
1 1/2 tsp	*SPICE BAZAAR MIDDLE EASTERN BLEND*
1 pint jar	grape leaves
2 Tbsp	butter, melted
1/4 cup	lemon juice

Filling: Place the rice and water in a small saucepan. Bring to a boil. Reduce heat and simmer 7 to 10 minutes, until the water is absorbed. Transfer to a large bowl and let it cool slightly. Mix in meat, salt, pepper and *MIDDLE EASTERN BLEND.*

Roll Grape Leaves: Drain water from the jar of grape leaves and carefully remove leaves. Unroll each stack of leaves and cut off stems. Rinse under running warm water. Drain in a colander. Set aside 3 or 4 leaves to line the bottom of the pan. Lay several leaves on the table side by side, with the smooth, shiny side down and stem end facing you. Place 2 tsp filling on each leaf 1 inch down from the stem end. Press the rice mixture to about 1 1/2 inches long. Working from the stem end, fold leaf up and over filling, then fold the sides in and roll up. Continue filling and rolling the rest of the leaves.

Line the bottom of a medium saucepan with the reserved grape leaves. Place rolled grape leaves snugly side-by-side in the pot, seam side down, layer upon layer. Drizzle melted butter on top of the rolled grape leaves. Place an inverted plate on top of the grape leaves to hold them down while cooking. Add water just to the top of the leaves. Bring to a boil. Reduce heat and simmer, covered, for 30 minutes. Remove lid and plate and pour lemon juice on top. Replace plate, raise heat to a slow boil and continue cooking, uncovered, until most of the liquid is evaporated, about 10 minutes.

In the Middle East, stuffed grape leaves are traditionally served with plain yogurt or Tsatsiki (page 28). In Greece, they are cooked with less lemon juice and served with Avgolemono Sauce (page 21).

NOTES: When using fresh grape leaves, blanch them first. Add a little salt to the pot while blanching. Also, increase the lemon juice to 1/3 cup.

Cooked Dolmades freeze well and can be reheated in a steamer or microwave.

MALFOOF
(Cabbage Rolls)
Makes 30 to 40 rolls

Cabbage rolls take a little extra time to prepare, but they can be rolled and cooked a day before serving. The flavor actually improves with reheating.

Filling ingredients from Dolmades recipe (page 106)

1 8 oz can	tomato sauce
1/4 cup	lemon juice
1 clove	garlic, crushed
1 tsp	salt
1/2 tsp	*SPICE BAZAAR MIDDLE EASTERN BLEND*
1 large	head cabbage

Prepare filling according to instructions in Dolmades recipe and set aside.

In a small bowl, blend tomato sauce, lemon juice, crushed garlic, salt and *MIDDLE EASTERN BLEND*. Set aside.

Prepare Cabbage: Rinse cabbage and remove core. Place in a plastic bag, leaving end open. Place bag on a microwave-safe plate and microwave on high for 5 minutes. Turn and microwave 2 to 3 minutes more until leaves are softened. Carefully remove cabbage from bag (it will be very hot). Rinse under cold water. Separate leaves and cut the thick vein from the center of each leaf. Leave small leaves whole, cut medium leaves in half and large leaves in thirds. Place scraps of cabbage in the bottom of a large saucepan. If the inner leaves of the cabbage head are not softened enough, return to microwave for 2 to 3 minutes more, as needed.

Roll Cabbage: Place 1 to 1 1/2 Tbsp filling in the center of each leaf, pressing to about 2 inches long. Fold leaf over the filling, and then fold sides in and roll up. Place rolls snugly side-by-side in the pot, seam side down, layer upon layer.

Pour tomato sauce mixture over cabbage rolls. Place an inverted plate on top to hold them down while cooking. Add water up to the top of the cabbage rolls. Bring to a boil. Reduce heat and simmer, covered, for 30 minutes. Remove lid and raise heat to a slow boil. Continue cooking until most of the liquid has evaporated, 10 to 15 minutes more.

NOTE: If there is extra filling, prepare stuffed tomatoes to cook with the cabbage rolls. Cut tops off tomatoes and scoop out insides. Fill with rice and meat. Put tops back on tomatoes. Place in pan with the cabbage rolls.

LAMB OUZI
(Lamb and Rice Platter)
Makes 6 to 8 servings

This is a traditional special occasion main dish in Jordan, where a whole lamb is often prepared to serve large crowds. It is a beautiful presentation that will impress your guests.

1	double recipe Basmati Rice (page 38)
6 to 8 lb	leg of lamb
2 Tbsp	*SPICE BAZAAR DAMASCUS KIBBIE SPICE*
2 Tbsp	Clarified Butter (page 159)
1/4 cup	pine nuts
1/4 cup	blanched almonds
1/4 cup	each raw pistachios, white raisins and currants
1/2 lb	baby carrots
1/2 lb	frozen peas
4	eggs, hard boiled, peeled and cut in half

Have butcher trim fat from leg of lamb and cut into 2 inch slices the full length of the leg, including the shank. Cut the slices into large chunks. Place lamb and *DAMASCUS KIBBIE SPICE* in a large pot. Add water to cover and bring to a boil. Skim off foam. Reduce heat and simmer, covered, until tender about 45 minutes. Drain water from lamb and reserve for preparing Basmati Rice. Keep meat warm while preparing rice.

Prepare rice according to recipe on page 38, substituting the lamb broth for the water.

In a small frying pan, sauté pine nuts and almonds in Clarified Butter until golden brown. Stir in pistachios, white raisins and currants. Remove from heat and set aside. Steam carrots and peas separately in a small amount of water until tender crisp.

Arrange Platter: Spread rice on a large serving platter. Place lamb on top. Sprinkle nuts, white raisins and currants over lamb. Arrange carrots, peas and eggs around edge of platter.

Tsatsiki (page 28) and a tossed salad with Lebanese Dressing (page 27) round out this beautiful meal.

MADABA MEATLOAF
AND VEGETABLE CASSEROLE
Makes 4 to 6 servings

This is a variation of a favorite dish from Madaba, Jordan where my father and my husband were from.

Meat Ingredients:

1 lb	lean ground beef or lamb
1/4 cup	onions, finely diced
1/4 cup	chopped parsley
1/2 cup	plain bread crumbs
1/4 cup	white wine
1 Tbsp	SPICE BAZAAR DAMASCUS KIBBIE SPICE

Vegetables:

1/2 lb	baby carrots
1/4 cup	diced onion
2 medium	zucchini, sliced 1/4 inch thick
1 cup	mushrooms, cut in half or quarters

Sauce:

1 15 oz can	crushed tomatoes
1 cup	water
2 tsp	SPICE BAZAAR DAMASCUS KIBBIE SPICE

Preheat oven to 350 degrees. Spray a 9x13 inch baking pan with non-stick spray.

Place meat ingredients in a bowl and mix well. Press evenly in the bottom of the baking pan. Boil carrots in water to cover until half cooked, 5 to 7 minutes. Distribute carrots and remaining vegetables over meat. Mix the crushed tomatoes, water and 2 tsp *DAMASCUS KIBBIE SPICE* together in a bowl and pour over the vegetables. Cover tightly and bake 45 minutes, until vegetables are tender. Uncover and place under broiler until browned.

Serve over Syrian Rice (page 40), or for a one-dish meal add cubed potatoes with the vegetables.

MOROCCAN LAMB COUSCOUS
Makes 6 to 8 servings

1	double recipe Moroccan Couscous Pilaf (page 43)

2 lb	boneless leg of lamb, cut into 1 inch cubes
1 1/2 Tbsp	*SPICE BAZAAR MOROCCAN BLEND*
3 Tbsp	Clarified Butter (page 159)

1/2 lb	baby carrots
2 small	potatoes, peeled and cut into 1 inch cubes

1 15 oz can	small fava beans* or garbanzo beans
2 small	turnips, cut into 1/2 inch cubes
1/2 lb	zucchini, cut into 1/2 inch cubes
1/2 lb	banana squash, peeled and cut into 1/2 inch cubes
1/4 cup	chopped cilantro
1/4 cup	chopped parsley
1/2 cup	dried apricots, cut in half
1/4 cup	white raisins
1/4 cup	currants

1/4 cup	pine nuts or slivered almonds, toasted
1/4 cup	whole blanched almonds, toasted

Sprinkle lamb with *MOROCCAN BLEND*. Heat Clarified Butter in a large deep frying pan. Add the lamb and sauté over moderately high heat until browned. Add water to cover and bring to a boil. Reduce heat and simmer, covered, 30 minutes, until lamb is almost tender.

Add the baby carrots and potatoes to the pan and a little more water if needed. Cook about 10 minutes, until carrots and potatoes are half cooked. Then add the rest of the vegetables (and a little more water if needed) and cook 5 to 10 minutes until the vegetables are almost done. Add the apricots, raisins, currants, pine nuts and almonds. Again, add a little more water, if needed. Simmer for 5 minutes more. The secret of this recipe is to add small amounts of water at a time, as needed, so that the vegetables and lamb are always simmering in a rich, thick sauce.

To Serve: Spread Moroccan Couscous Pilaf on a large serving platter and top with the meat and vegetables. Pour sauce over all.

*See Glossary of Ingredients page 165.

JORDANIAN TAJIN
(Oven-baked Lamb Stew)
Makes 6 servings

1 1/2 lb	boneless leg of lamb or lamb shoulder, cut into 1inch cubes
2 Tbsp	olive oil
2 tsp	*SPICE BAZAAR JORDANIAN ROAST LAMB SPICE*
2	medium potatoes, peeled and cut into 1 inch pieces
2	carrots, peeled and cut into 1/2 inch pieces
1	medium zucchini, cut into 1 inch pieces
6 to 8	medium mushrooms, cut in half
1 rib	celery, cut into 1/2 inch pieces
1 large	onion, cut into large chunks
1/4 cup	chopped parsley
1 15 oz can	diced tomatoes
1 Tbsp	*SPICE BAZAAR JORDANIAN ROAST LAMB SPICE*

Spray a 9x13 inch baking pan with non-stick spray.

Heat olive oil in a medium saucepan. Add lamb and 2 tsp *JORDANIAN ROAST LAMB SPICE*. Sauté over moderately high heat, stirring frequently, until meat is browned. Add water to cover and bring to a boil. Reduce heat and simmer, covered, for about 30 minutes, until meat is almost tender. Add a little more water if needed.

While meat is cooking, prepare the vegetables and place them in the baking pan. Place the cooked meat and broth on top of the vegetables. Pour the canned tomatoes on top and sprinkle with 1 Tbsp *JORDANIAN ROAST LAMB SPICE*. Cover tightly and bake in a 400 degree oven for 45 minutes, or until vegetables and meat are tender. Uncover and raise heat to 475 degrees. Add a little water to pan if juices have dried out. Bake 15 minutes longer, until vegetables and meat have browned.

This hearty stew is traditionally served over Syrian Rice (page 40) along with a simple tossed salad.

MOUSSAKA
(Greek Eggplant and Meat Casserole)
Makes 8 to 10 servings

This classic Greek dish is perfect for entertaining. Because it is
prepared ahead, you will enjoy more time with your guests and spend
less time in the kitchen. Follow the steps for preparation in the order
given and it will go together smoothly and easily. As you complete
each step, take a minute to clean up the cooking utensils used and your
final cleanup will be much easier. You can also prepare the meat sauce
and the cheese sauce a day ahead if convenient. If desired, you can
substitute 2 lb zucchini for the eggplant.

Meat Sauce:

1 1/2 lb	lean ground beef or lamb
1 cup	diced onion
2 cloves	garlic, crushed
1/4 cup	red wine
1/2 cup	plain bread crumbs
1/2 cup	chopped parsley
1 cup	water
1 15 oz can	crushed tomatoes
2 1/2 Tbsp	SPICE BAZAAR GREEK SALAD DRESSING BLEND

Potatoes and Eggplant:

4 medium	potatoes, peeled and cut into 1/4 inch slices
2 medium	eggplants, cut into 1/2 inch round slices
1/4 cup	olive oil
	SPICE BAZAAR GREEK SALAD DRESSING BLEND

Cheese Sauce:

1/3 cup	butter
1/3 cup	flour
1 tsp	SPICE BAZAAR RANDA'S SPICE
3 cups	milk
2	eggs
1 cup	grated mizethra* or Parmesan cheese

Additional Ingredients for Assembly:

2 Tbsp	butter, melted
1/2 cup	bread crumbs
	SPICE BAZAAR GREEK SALAD DRESSING BLEND
	ground nutmeg

Preheat oven to broil. Spray a 10x14 inch baking pan with non-stick spray.

Meat Sauce: Cook meat, onion and garlic in a large saucepan, until lightly browned. Add the remaining meat sauce ingredients and simmer for 10 to 15 minutes, adding a little water if it is too thick. It should be like a thick spaghetti sauce.

Potatoes and Eggplant: Place sliced potatoes in boiling water to cover and simmer until done, but still firm, about 5 to 7 minutes. Drain and set aside. Line a shallow baking pan with foil. Drizzle with olive oil. Place eggplant slices on pan and turn to coat both sides with oil. Sprinkle with *GREEK SALAD DRESSING BLEND.* Place under broiler for 5 minutes on each side, until browned. Set aside. Immediately turn down oven temperature to 350 degrees.

Cheese Sauce: Melt butter in a medium saucepan over medium heat. Add flour and *RANDA'S SPICE,* whisking briskly until thick and bubbly. Remove from heat and gradually whisk in the milk. Return to heat and bring to a boil, stirring constantly. Reduce heat and simmer 1 to 2 minutes, until sauce thickens. Remove from heat again. Place eggs in a bowl and beat thoroughly. Slowly pour 1 cup sauce into eggs, beating continuously. Pour egg mixture into remaining sauce, whisking continuously. Heat just until it comes to a boil. Stir in half of the cheese, reserving the rest for later.

Assembly: Drizzle 2 Tbsp melted butter in baking pan and spread with 1/2 cup bread crumbs. Sprinkle crumbs with *GREEK SALAD DRESSING BLEND.* Lay potato slices on top of crumbs. Spread meat sauce over the potatoes. Place eggplant slices over meat sauce. Then pour cheese sauce on top. Sprinkle with reserved grated cheese and a little nutmeg. Bake in a 350 degree oven for 40 to 50 minutes, until cheese sauce is browned. Allow Moussaka to set for 10 to 15 minutes before cutting into squares and serving.

Moussaka can be prepared ahead and refrigerated or frozen unbaked. If frozen, allow an extra 45 minutes to bake.

*See Glossary of Ingredients page 166.

PASTICCIO
(Greek Macaroni and Meat Casserole)
Makes 8 to 10 servings

As with Moussaka, the secret to easy preparation is assembling all of the ingredients before beginning and completing the sections one at a time in the order given.

1 lb	Greek macaroni #1 or #2* (if these are not available, substitute ziti or mostaccioli pasta)

White Sauce:

3 Tbsp	butter
3 Tbsp	flour
2 cups	milk
2 tsp	SPICE BAZAAR RANDA'S SPICE

1 recipe	Meat Sauce from Moussaka (page 112)
1 recipe	Cheese Sauce from Moussaka (page 112)

Preheat oven to 350 degrees. Spray a 10x14 inch baking pan with non-stick spray.

Cook macaroni according to package directions, taking care not to overcook. Drain, rinse in cold water and place in a large bowl. While macaroni is cooking, prepare the White Sauce.

White Sauce: In a medium saucepan, melt butter and whisk in flour and *RANDA'S SPICE*. Remove from heat and gradually whisk in milk. Return to heat and bring to a boil, stirring constantly. Simmer 1 minute. The sauce should be fairly thin. Pour over drained macaroni and gently mix in.

Assembly: Place half of the macaroni in the baking pan. Spread the meat sauce over the macaroni. Place the rest of the macaroni over the meat sauce. Spread the cheese sauce on top and sprinkle with reserved grated cheese. Bake for 40 to 50 minutes, until cheese sauce is browned. Let it set for 10 to 15 minutes before cutting into squares and serving.

Pasticcio can be made ahead and refrigerated or frozen unbaked. Allow 45 minutes extra baking time if frozen.

*See Glossary of Ingredients page 165.

KEFTEDES IN WINE SAUCE
(Greek Meatballs in Wine Sauce)
Makes 5 to 6 servings

Sauce:

3 8 oz cans	tomato sauce
2 Tbsp	*SPICE BAZAAR HELLENIC HERB BLEND*
1 cup	red wine

Meatballs:

1 lb	lean ground beef or lamb
1/4 cup	finely chopped parsley
1/2 cup	finely minced onion
1/2 cup	plain bread crumbs
1/4 cup	red wine
1	egg, slightly beaten
2 Tbsp	*SPICE BAZAAR HELLENIC HERB BLEND*

Place sauce ingredients in a bowl and stir to blend. Set aside.

Place meatball ingredients in a bowl and mix thoroughly. Shape into 1 inch balls. Spray a large, deep frying pan with non-stick spray and sauté the Keftedes until browned. Pour prepared sauce over the Keftedes and bring to a boil. Reduce heat and simmer, uncovered, for 10 to 15 minutes until sauce is thick.

Serve over Orzo with Feta (page 43) or Syrian Rice (page 40).

GRECIAN LAMB SHANKS WITH WHITE BEANS
Makes 4 servings

4	lamb shanks
1 15 oz can	white beans, with juice
1 large	onion, sliced
4 cloves	garlic, sliced
2 Tbsp	*SPICE BAZAAR GREEK SALAD DRESSING BLEND*
1/4 cup	chopped parsley
1 15 oz can	crushed tomatoes

Preheat oven to 375 degrees. Spray a 9 x 13 inch baking pan with non-stick spray.

Trim lamb shanks of excess fat. Pour canned beans into the baking pan. Place shanks on top of the beans. Distribute onion and garlic slices over the lamb shanks. Sprinkle with *GREEK SALAD DRESSING BLEND* and chopped parsley. Pour crushed tomatoes over all. Cover tightly and bake for 1 1/2 to 2 hours, until lamb is very tender. Add water as needed to keep it from drying out.

The rich, flavorful sauce with the beans is excellent served over Orzo with Feta (page 43) or Syrian Rice (page 40).

JORDANIAN SCRAMBLED EGGS WITH MEAT
Makes 8 to 10 servings

We serve this easily prepared egg dish for holiday breakfasts and brunches. Because it contains meat, it eliminates the need to prepare bacon or sausages and is always a big hit.

1/2 lb	lean ground beef or lamb
1/2 cup	diced onion
1 Tbsp	*SPICE BAZAAR JORDANIAN ROAST LAMB SPICE*
12	eggs

In a large non-stick frying pan sauté meat, onion and *JORDANIAN ROAST LAMB SPICE* until meat is browned. Crack eggs into a bowl and beat lightly. Pour eggs over meat. Cook over medium heat, stirring gently until eggs are set.

ORANGE-GLAZED HAM STEAKS
Makes 4 servings

With this recipe you can enjoy the flavor of slow-baked ham in less than 10 minutes for a quick and easy entrée.

1 Tbsp	butter
2 Tbsp	honey
2 Tbsp	frozen orange juice concentrate
1/4 tsp	ground cloves
2 tsp	*SPICE BAZAAR SHAFIK'S RED LENTIL SOUP SPICE*
4	ham steaks, 4 oz each

In a large frying pan, melt butter and add the remaining ingredients, except ham steaks. Simmer 1 minute. Add the ham steaks and cook over medium heat 2 minutes on each side, until well browned and glazed.

BREADS

◆ Denotes Vegetarian
✖ Denotes Vegan/Lenten

NOTES ON YEAST

My recipes call for fast rising yeast. It is easier to use because it does not have to be dissolved in water, but is added directly to the flour. It also uses a much warmer water temperature. When using regular active dry yeast or fresh yeast follow package instructions. The rising time will be longer than indicated in the instructions. With any type of yeast, the exact quantity of flour and the water temperature may vary according to the climate and the temperature of your kitchen. If you live in a damp climate, you may need to add more flour. Have all ingredients at room temperature. Dough rises best in a warm kitchen, so adjust you kitchen temperature accordingly. In dry climates the cloth covering the dough can be sprayed lightly with water to keep dough moist. 1 package of fast rising yeast or active dry yeast (1/4 oz) equals about 2 1/4 tsp.

ZATAR PITA CHIPS ❖

Serves ??? (depends on if you can stop munching)

6	pitas
1 tsp	**SPICE BAZAAR RANDA'S SPICE**
1/2 cup	mixed zatar*
2 Tbsp	olive oil

Preheat oven to 350 degrees.

In a small bowl, mix **RANDA'S SPICE** and the zatar. Split pitas open and cut into small wedges. Place on a baking sheet with insides facing up. Sprinkle with the zatar mix. Drizzle with olive oil. Bake for 10 to 15 minutes until crisp.

Zatar Pita Chips are great served with Hummus (page 10).

*See Glossary of Ingredients page 166.

FETA AND HERB BREAD ◆

Makes 6 pitas

1/4 lb	crumbled feta cheese (about 1 cup)
2 Tbsp	olive oil
2 tsp	*SPICE BAZAAR HELLENIC HERB BLEND*
6	pitas

Mix feta, olive oil and Hellenic Herb Blend in a bowl. Add water, 1 tsp at a time if needed, to thin to spreading consistency. Spread 1 1/2 Tbsp on the bottom side of each pita. Place under a preheated broiler and broil until lightly browned.

MANAEESH ✤
(Zatar Herb Bread)

Makes 6 pitas

This short-cut version of a popular Middle Eastern breakfast and snack bread is ready in a few minutes. If you want to make it from scratch, prepare the Pita Bread recipe (page 124) and spread the zatar mixture over the loaves before baking.

1/2 cup	mixed zatar*
1 tsp	*SPICE BAZAAR RANDA'S SPICE*
1/4 cup	olive oil
6	pitas

Place zatar, *RANDA'S SPICE* and olive oil in a small bowl and mix. Stir in 1 to 2 tsp water to thin to spreading consistency. Spread 1 1/2 Tbsp on the bottom side of each pita. Place under a preheated broiler and broil until lightly browned.

*See Glossary of Ingredients (page 165).

SESAME GARLIC FRENCH BREAD ✤

1/3 cup	olive oil or butter, melted
1 to 2 cloves	garlic, crushed
2 Tbsp	sesame seeds
1 loaf	French bread

Preheat oven to broil.

In a small bowl, blend oil or butter and crushed garlic. Mix in sesame seeds. Cut bread in half lengthwise. Spread both cut surfaces with garlic butter. Sprinkle with one of the *SPICE BAZAAR BLENDS* below*. Place under broiler for a few minutes until toasted.

ETHIOPIAN HOT SPICE, HELLENIC HERB BLEND, ATHENIAN GARDEN SPICE, OR HERBES DE FRANCE

FATAYER DOUGH ✤
(Meat and Spinach Pie Dough)
Makes 20 individual pies

Dough:

4 to 4 1/2 cups	bread flour (Gold Medal Better for Bread®)
1 1/2 tsp	salt
1 Tbsp	sugar
1 pkg	fast rising (rapid rise) yeast
1/4 cup	salad oil
1 1/2 cups	very warm water (115 to 120 degrees)

Before beginning, see **NOTES ON YEAST** (page 119).

Prepare Dough: Mix 4 cups flour, salt, sugar and yeast in a large bowl. With a wooden spoon, stir in the oil and water to form a soft dough. Place dough on a lightly floured surface. Knead 5 to 7 minutes, until smooth and elastic, adding more flour as needed to keep dough from sticking. The kneading can also be done in an electric mixer using the dough hook attachment. Knead on low speed for 3 to 4 minutes. Place the dough in an oiled bowl and turn to coat both sides. Cover with a cloth and then with a large towel. Let it rise in a warm, draft-free place 25 to 35 minutes, until doubled in size.

Shape Dough: When dough has risen, remove from bowl and shape into a log about 20 inches long. Cut into 20 equal pieces. Shape each piece into a ball and place on a lightly floured cloth (an old pillowcase works well.). If dough is sticky, dust balls lightly with flour as you shape them. Cover balls with waxed paper or parchment and then with a towel. Let them rest for 20 to 25 minutes until almost doubled in size.

Line two large shallow baking pans with parchment or foil and drizzle with 3 Tbsp oil each.

Preheat oven to 375 degrees. With a rolling pin, roll each ball into a circle about 5 inches in diameter. Place a scant 1/4 cup of filling from the selected recipe (pages 122 and 123) on each circle. Bring edges of dough up and pinch closed to form a triangle. If the pie doesn't stay closed, dip a finger in water and dab lightly on the edges, then pinch closed. Place 10 pies on each baking tray.

Bake Pies: Bake for 20 minutes. Remove pies from oven and brush lightly with additional oil. Return to oven and continue baking 20 to 25 minutes until pies are browned. Transfer to a rack to cool.

NOTE: Baked Fatayer freeze well. Defrost and reheat in a 350 degree oven or in a microwave.

SPINACH FATAYER ✤
(Spinach Pies)
Makes 20 pies

1 recipe   Fatayer Dough (page 121)

Filling:
3 10 oz pkg	frozen chopped spinach, defrosted
1/4 cup	olive oil
3/4 cup	diced onion
2 Tbsp	SPICE BAZAAR SESAME TAHINI SAUCE AND DIP SPICE

Prepare Fatayer Dough and set aside to rise. While dough is rising, prepare the filling. Squeeze excess liquid from the spinach and place in a medium bowl. Mix in the remaining filling ingredients. Set aside until dough is ready. Then proceed with directions for shaping and baking pies.

POTATO AND MUSHROOM FATAYER ✤
Makes 20 pies

These delicious vegetarian pies are equally good with the *TANDOORI BOMBAY BLEND* or the *JORDANIAN ROAST LAMB SPICE.*

1 recipe	Fatayer Dough (page 121)
2 medium	potatoes, scrubbed and diced
1 16 oz can	garbanzos, drained and coarsely chopped
1 lb medium	mushrooms, quartered
2 cloves	garlic, minced
2 cups	diced onion
1 Tbsp	SPICE BAZAAR JORDANIAN ROAST LAMB SPICE **OR** SPICE BAZAAR TANDOORI BOMBAY BLEND

Prepare Fatayer Dough and set aside to rise. While dough is rising, cook the potatoes in boiling water to cover until done. Drain and place in a bowl. Mix in the remaining filling ingredients. Set aside until dough is ready. Then proceed with directions for shaping and baking pies.

MEAT FATAYER
(Meat Pies)
Makes 20 pies

1 recipe   Fatayer Dough (page 121)

Filling:

1 lb	lean ground beef or lamb
1/2 cup	chopped parsley
1/2 cup	finely diced onion
1/4 cup	pine nuts or slivered almonds, toasted
1/4 cup	plain bread crumbs
1 medium	tomato, diced
1 Tbsp	pomegranate syrup*
1 1/2 tsp	salt
1/2 tsp	pepper
2 1/2 tsp	*SPICE BAZAAR MIDDLE EASTERN BLEND*

Prepare Fatayer Dough and set aside to rise. While dough is rising, mix all filling ingredients in a medium bowl. Set aside until dough is ready. Then proceed with directions for shaping and baking pies.

Variation: Use filling ingredients above, substituting 1/2 cup sesame tahini paste or labany (yogurt cheese) for the tomato and pomegranate syrup.

See Glossary of Ingredients page 166.

PITA BREAD ✣
(Arabic Pocket Bread)
Makes 12 pitas

Pita bread is fun to bake and watch as it puffs up to form a pocket.
Start with this small recipe until you get comfortable with the baking
procedure. Then you can double the recipe to make a larger batch.

4-4 1/2 cups	bread flour (Gold Medal Better for Bread®)
1 1/2 tsp	salt
1 Tbsp	sugar
1 pkg	fast rising (rapid rise) yeast
1 3/4 cups	very warm water (115 to 120 degrees)
	pizza stone (available in most kitchen supply stores or department stores)

Before beginning, see NOTES ON YEAST (page 119)

Prepare Dough: Mix 4 cups flour, salt, sugar and yeast in a large
bowl. With a wooden spoon, stir in the water to form a soft dough.
Place dough on a lightly floured surface. Knead 5 to 7 minutes, until
smooth and elastic, adding more flour as needed to keep dough from
sticking. The kneading can also be done in an electric mixer using the
dough hook attachment. Knead on low speed for 4 to 5 minutes. Place
the dough in an oiled bowl and turn to coat both sides. Cover with a
cloth and then with a thick towel. Let it rise in a warm place 25 to 35
minutes, until doubled in size.

Shape Dough: When dough has risen, punch it down and knead out the
air bubbles. Remove it from bowl and shape into a log about 15 inches
long. Cut into 12 equal pieces. Shape each piece into a ball and place
on a lightly floured cloth (an old pillowcase works well.). If dough is
sticky, dust balls lightly with flour as you shape them. Cover balls with
waxed paper or parchment and then with a towel. Let them rest for
20 to 25 minutes until almost doubled in size.

When the balls have risen, place the pizza stone on the lowest rack in
the oven and the other rack 3 to 4 inches from the top of the oven.
Preheat to 450 degrees. On a lightly floured board, roll out the balls
with a rolling pin to about 5 or 6 inches in diameter. They should be
thin, no more than 1/8 inch. Place the pitas back on the lightly floured
cloth. Cover with wax paper or parchment and then with a towel. Let
them rest for 20 to 25 minutes until almost doubled.

Bake Bread: For easy access to the pizza stone when ready to bake, pull the oven rack out. Gently transfer the first loaf to the palm of your hand, keeping your palm flat. Slide the loaf off of your hand and onto the pizza stone. Be careful to avoid touching the stone, as it is very hot. Place one or two more loaves on the pizza stone. Bake for about 5 minutes, until the bread is lightly browned on the bottom. If the loaves are still too white on the top, place them directly on the top rack of the oven to brown for 30 to 60 seconds. Transfer the baked loaves to a cooling rack and cover with a towel. Place two or three more pitas in the oven and continue the baking procedure until all the loaves are baked. Pack the baked pitas in a plastic bag while still slightly warm.

NOTE: It is important to be very gentle when lifting the risen loaves and placing them in the oven, or they will not form the pockets.

SUGGESTION: For variety, prepare some of the mixture for Zatar Herb Bread (page 120) or Feta and Herb Bread (page 120) and spread it on the loaves before baking.

GARDEN PIZZA ◆

Makes 2 12 inch pizzas

Homemade pizza is quick and easy with this simplified recipe. While the dough is rising, prepare the sauce and vegetables. Using fast rising yeast, the pizza will be ready in little over an hour.

Dough:

1 pkg	fast rising (rapid rise) dry yeast
3 1/3 to 4 cups	flour
1 tsp	salt
1 Tbsp	sugar
2 Tbsp	olive oil
1 1/4 cups	very warm water (115 to 120 degrees)

Sauce:

2 8 oz cans	tomato sauce
1/4 cup	grated Parmesan cheese
4 tsp	*SPICE BAZAAR HELLENIC HERB BLEND*

Toppings:

12 oz	mozzarella cheese, grated
2 small	zucchini or crooked neck squash, thinly sliced
2 6 oz jars	marinated artichoke hearts
1 cup	thinly sliced onion
1 cup	thinly sliced mushrooms
1 medium	green bell pepper, thinly sliced
1 medium	red pepper, thinly sliced
1/4 cup	pine nuts
1/4 cup	capers

Oil 2 pizza pans or cookie trays with 1 tsp olive oil each.

Before beginning, see NOTES ON YEAST (page 119).

Prepare Pizza Dough: Mix yeast, 3 cups flour, salt and sugar in a large bowl. Add the olive oil and water and beat until smooth. Gradually add more flour until dough is too stiff to stir. Turn dough out onto a lightly floured table. Knead until smooth and elastic, about 5 to 7 minutes. Dust with more flour as needed to keep the dough from sticking. The kneading can also be done in an electric mixer using the dough hook attachment. Knead on low speed for 3 to 4 minutes. Place the dough in an oiled bowl and turn dough to coat both sides. Cover with a cloth and then with a thick towel. Let it rise in a warm place 25 to 35 minutes, until doubled in size. When dough is almost ready, preheat oven to 500 degrees (a very hot oven works best).

Shape Pizza Dough: Place half of the dough on each baking sheet and press out to a 12 inch circle. Pinch up the edges to make a rim. Bake 10 minutes, until lightly browned.

Prepare Sauce and Assemble Pizza: Mix sauce ingredients in a small saucepan and simmer for 1 to 2 minutes. Spread half of the sauce on each of the two lightly browned crusts. Place mozzarella on top of the sauce and then distribute the toppings over the cheese. Bake 10 to 15 minutes more until the cheese is melted and the crust is well browned.

PITA PIZZAS ◆
Makes 6 individual pizzas

This recipe is great for quick pizzas.

Sauce:

1 8 oz can	tomato sauce
2 Tbsp	grated Parmesan cheese
2 tsp	SPICE BAZAAR HELLENIC HERB BLEND
6	pitas
6 oz	mozzarella cheese, grated
	toppings of your choice*

Preheat oven to 450 degrees.

Mix sauce ingredients in a small pan and simmer for 1 to 2 minutes. Place pitas on a cookie sheet, bottom side up. Spread the sauce on the pitas. Then sprinkle with the grated mozzarella. Distribute toppings over the cheese.

Bake for 5 to 10 minutes until cheese is melted and toppings are browned.

Topping Suggestions: Thinly sliced vegetables (green bell peppers, red bell peppers, mushrooms, onions), black olives, anchovies, pepperoni, diced ham or whatever your family likes.

For a memorable and easy children's birthday party, have the sauce, cheese and an assortment of toppings ready and let each child make his or her own pizza. Pita Pizza parties are always a big hit.

TSOUREKI ♦
(Greek Easter Bread)
Makes 2 loaves

This mildly sweet and deliciously flavored, fragrant bread is a special treat after a long Lenten season. It is especially good toasted and buttered.

5 to 6 cups	bread flour (Gold Medal Better for Bread®)
1/4 tsp	mistika (gum mastic)*
1 tsp	sugar
1/2 tsp	ground mahlab (mahlapi)*
2/3 cup	sugar
1/2 tsp	salt
2 pkgs	fast rising (rapid rise) yeast
1 1/3 cups	very warm milk (115 to 120 degrees)
1/2 cup	butter, softened
1	egg
1 tsp	vanilla

Glaze:

1	egg
2 Tbsp	water
2 Tbsp	sesame seeds
2	red Easter eggs

Before beginning, see NOTES ON YEAST (page 119)

Spray a large baking tray with non-stick spray.

Mix Ingredients: Place 5 cups of flour in a large bowl. Set 1 cup aside to be added as needed if the dough is too soft. Place the mistika and 1 tsp sugar in a mortar and pestle and crush to a powder. Or place them between 2 layers of plastic wrap and slap sharply several times with the flat side of a large knife blade. Stir the mistika, mahlab, sugar, salt and yeast into the flour. Make a well in the center of the flour and add the milk, butter, egg and vanilla, working them in until all is incorporated.

Knead Dough: Place the dough on a lightly floured surface and knead 5 to 7 minutes until smooth and elastic. The dough should be fairly soft. The kneading can also be done in an electric mixer. Place the dough in the mixer bowl and attach the dough hook. Knead for 3 to 4 minutes on low speed, until smooth and elastic. Stop a couple of times to push the dough down from the hook. With either method, if the dough is sticky, dust lightly with flour as needed. Place the dough in a bowl and cover with a cloth and then with a thick towel. Set it aside in a warm, draft-free place to rise until doubled in size, 50 to 60 minutes.

Shape Bread: When the dough has risen, punch it down and knead out the air bubbles. Cover and let the dough rest for about 10 minutes and then divide it in half. *To make 2 braided loaves:* divide each half into 3 parts and roll each part into a rope about 10 inches long. Braid the three ropes together and pinch the ends to seal. Turn the pinched ends under. Repeat with the other half of the dough. *To make round loaves:* simply shape each half of the dough into a smooth ball. Place the shaped loaves on the baking tray. Cover with waxed paper or parchment and then with a towel. Set aside in a warm, draft-free place to rise until almost double, about 35 to 45 minutes. This is a rich, sweet dough and takes longer than other doughs to rise, so be patient.

Bake Bread: When the dough is almost ready, preheat the oven to 325 degrees. When the bread is ready to bake, prepare the glaze by beating the egg and water in a small bowl. Dip your fingers in the glaze and gently spread it over the surface of each loaf. Sprinkle each loaf with 1 Tbsp sesame seeds. Bake for 40 to 50 minutes until browned. Transfer to a cooling rack. After the bread has cooled for 20 to 30 minutes, cut a small hole in the center of each loaf and press in the red egg.

*See Glossary of Ingredients page 166.

VASILOPITA ◆
(Greek New Year's Bread)

Vasilopita is the same basic bread as Tsoureki. Instead of the Easter egg, it has a coin baked in the middle. Tradition says that the person who gets the coin when the bread is sliced gets special good luck for the New Year.

Follow instructions for preparing the dough and shaping bread in the Tsoureki (page 128). After the loaves have been shaped, cut a slit in the bottom of each loaf and insert a coin, which has been wrapped in foil. Continue with the rising and baking instructions in the Tsoureki recipe.

TALAMEE ✤
(Syrian Bread)
Makes 4 nine inch loaves

I have happy memories from my childhood of my mother baking these round, flat loaves. On baking days there was no need for her to cook dinner. All we wanted was to feast on the fresh baked bread slathered with butter and jam. Now I bake for my grandchildren. My eldest grandson, Peter, can eat a whole loaf in one sitting. He says, "It goes down so easy."

2 1/2 lb	bread flour (Gold Medal Better for Bread®)
2 pkg	fast rising (rapid rise) yeast
2 Tbsp	sugar
1 Tbsp	salt
3 cups	very warm water (115 to 120 degrees)
2 Tbsp	vegetable oil

Before beginning, see NOTES ON YEAST (page 119).

Mix Ingredients: Place all but 1 cup of the flour in a large bowl. Set the cup of flour aside to be added as needed if the dough is too soft. Mix in the yeast, sugar and salt. Add the oil to the water. Make a well in the center of the flour and gradually add the water and oil, working it in until all is incorporated.

Knead Dough: Place the dough on a lightly floured surface and knead 5 to 7 minutes until smooth and elastic. The dough should be fairly stiff. Dust with more flour, as needed, to keep the dough from sticking. The kneading can also be done in an electric mixer. **In this case, use cooler water, 90 to 95 degrees.** Place the ingredients in the mixer bowl and attach the dough hook. Knead for 3 to 4 minutes on low speed, until smooth and elastic. Stop a couple of times to push the dough down from the hook. Shape into a ball and place in an oiled bowl, smooth side up. Cover with a cloth and then with a thick towel. Let it rise in a warm, draft-free place until doubled in size, 35 to 45 minutes.

Shape Dough: When the dough is ready, punch it down, knead out air bubbles and divide it into four portions. Shape each portion into a smooth, round ball and place on a floured cloth at least 2 inches apart. Cover with waxed paper or parchment and then with a towel. Let the balls rest for about 20 to 30 minutes until almost double in size.

While the balls are resting, line 2 12x18 inch baking trays or 2 large cookie sheets with parchment or spray with non-stick spray and set aside. When the balls are ready, press them flat with your fingers and then roll out to a diameter of 9 to 10 inches. Place two loaves on each tray. Again, cover the loaves with wax paper or parchment and then the towel. Let the loaves rise until almost double, about 15 to 20 minutes. While the loaves are rising, preheat the oven to 375 degrees.

Bake Bread: When the loaves have risen, place the trays in the oven and bake for 20 minutes. Rotate the trays after 10 minutes for even baking. When they are lightly browned, transfer them to a cooling rack. When the loaves have cooled thoroughly, pack them in plastic bags. Extra Talamee may be stored in the freezer.

SUGGESTIONS:
- To make eight loaves, double all the ingredients, except the yeast. Use three packages of yeast. If you wish to use your mixer for kneading, knead half of the dough at a time.

- This dough makes excellent pizza crust, so treat your family to some pizza on bread baking days. (See page 126 for an easy sauce recipe and topping suggestions.)

- Vary the bread by baking some in loaf pans or making round, thick loaves that can be sliced for sandwiches.

ORTHODOX CHURCH HOLY BREAD ✣
Makes 4 loaves

This bread, also called, **QURBAN** in Arabic and **PROSPHORON** in Greek is used in Orthodox church services.

2 1/2 lb	bread flour (Gold Medal Better for Bread®)
1 pkg	fast rising (rapid rise) yeast
3 1/4 cups	very warm water (115 to 120 degrees)
	Holy Bread Stamp*

Before beginning, see NOTES ON YEAST (page 119).

Mix Ingredients: Place flour in a large bowl and mix in yeast. Make a well in the center of the flour and gradually add the water, working it in until all is incorporated. Follow the *Knead Dough* instructions in the Talamee recipe (page 130),

Shape Dough: When the dough has risen, **preheat oven to 325 degrees**. Punch down the risen dough and knead out the air bubbles. Divide into 4 portions and shape each portion into a smooth, round ball. Place on a floured cloth at least 2 inches apart. Cover with waxed paper or parchment and then a towel. Let rest for about 10 minutes so the dough will relax. Spray 2 12x18 inch baking trays with non-stick spray. Place 2 balls on each tray. Press them flat to about 1/2 inch. If they don't flatten easily, cover with a cloth and wait five minutes so the dough will relax more. Lightly flour the tops of the flattened loaves and distribute the flour evenly. Firmly and evenly press the Holy Bread stamp in the center of each loaf to imprint the seal. Gently lift stamp off loaf at an angle (lifting straight up can cause an unclear impression). Make several pricks with a wooden skewer or thin straw at the corners of the cross in the seal and then make several more pricks on the loaf in the area not stamped with the seal. These pricks help prevent air bubbles from forming.

Bake Bread: **Immediately after stamping** place trays in the oven and bake for 25 to 35 minutes. Rotate trays after 15 minutes for even baking. When loaves are lightly browned, transfer them to a cooling rack. Wipe off the tops with a damp cloth. While the loaves are still a little warm, wrap them tightly in plastic wrap. A tight wrap will prevent any ice crystals from forming if the bread is to be frozen.

SUGGESTION: If you do not have enough trays, you can let the rolled-out loaves rest on the floured cloth until the first 2 trays have been removed from the oven. Then, cool the trays down and gently transfer two unbaked loaves to each tray.

NOTE: This recipe uses only flour, water and yeast, which is the traditional way to prepare Holy Bread. However, you can add 2 tsp sugar and 3/4 tsp salt to help the dough develop.

*See Glossary of Ingredients (page 165).

DESSERTS

RICE PUDDING
Makes 5 1-cup servings

This rice pudding is enormously popular at the Middle Eastern Bakery & Deli where it was developed. The hint of orange flower water gives a unique flavor that makes this pudding sophisticated comfort food.

1 1/2 cups	water
1/3 cup	calrose (pearl or medium grain) rice
1/3 cup	corn starch
1/3 cup	sugar
1 tsp	vanilla
1/4 tsp	orange flower water*
	Pinch of salt
4 cups	whole or 2% milk,** divided
	ground cinnamon

Place the water and rice in a large microwave-safe bowl. Microwave on high for about 10 to 12 minutes until the water is completely absorbed and the rice is very soft. Stir in the cornstarch, sugar, vanilla, orange flower water and 1 cup of the milk. Set aside.

Place the remaining 3 cups of milk in a medium saucepan. Bring to a full boil over medium heat, stirring frequently to prevent scorching. Remove from heat and stir in the rice mixture. Return to medium heat and cook, stirring constantly, until the mixture comes to a full boil. Continue cooking **without stirring** for 1 minute. The pudding will appear thin, but will thicken after it is chilled. Stir once and pour into individual bowls and refrigerate. Sprinkle with cinnamon before serving.

NOTE: It is important to minimize stirring the pudding after it has thickened or it may break down and become watery.

*See Glossary of Ingredients page 166.

** If you prefer nonfat milk, use an extra tablespoon of cornstarch.

BAKLAVA
(Filo and Walnut Pastry)
Makes 12 x 18 inch pan

Baklava is the most popular dessert in the entire Mediterranean area. If you have never worked with filo dough, be sure to read the instructions on Handling Filo Dough (page 161). You will be pleasantly surprised at how easy it can be to use.

1 3/4 cups	melted Clarified Butter (page 159), divided
5 cups	chopped walnuts
1/2 cup	sugar
1/2 tsp	cinnamon
1/4 tsp	cloves
1/4 tsp	nutmeg
2 lb	12x17" filo dough, defrosted (see Handling Filo Dough, page 161)
1 recipe	Basic Syrup, cooled (page 137)

Preheat oven to 325 degrees. Brush a 12 x 18 inch baking pan with 2 Tbsp Clarified Butter

Mix walnuts with the sugar and spices in a bowl. Set aside. Place two sheets of filo dough in the buttered pan. Brush generously with Clarified Butter. Place two more sheets in the pan and brush with Clarified Butter again. Repeat this procedure until all but four sheets of the first package of filo dough are used up. Lay two sheets, lengthwise, across the narrow half of the pan with edges of the dough overhanging the edges of the pan. Lay the last two sheets on the other half of the pan, again with the dough overhanging the edges. Spread the walnuts evenly over the dough. Turn the edges of the dough in to enclose the walnuts.

Using the second package of filo dough, repeat the layering and buttering procedure until all of the dough is used. Pour any leftover butter on top of the Baklava. Using a sharp knife, cut the Baklava into four equally spaced rows lengthwise. Be sure to cut through almost all of the layers of dough on these first cuts so that the syrup will soak to the bottom after the Baklava is baked. Then cut into six rows widthwise. Next, cut at an angle across the rows to form triangles.

Bake for 1 1/4 to 1 1/2 hours until golden brown. Ovens vary, so if the dough is browning on top too quickly before the under layers of filo can bake, reduce the temperature by 25 degrees.

When the Baklava is baked, remove it from the oven and slowly pour the cooled syrup over the top. Set it aside and let it cool thoroughly. Before serving, use a sharp knife to cut the pieces apart.

NOTES: The size pan used in this recipe is a standard half sheet pan, which is available at restaurant and kitchen supply stores. Disposable half-sheet pans are also available in many supermarkets. If you use a different size pan, cut the stack of filo to fit the pan before buttering and placing in the pan. Scrap pieces can be used in the middle of the Baklava.

Baked Baklava may be wrapped in plastic wrap and frozen for future use. Before serving, let it defrost, covered, for about one hour.

BASIC SYRUP
Makes 3 cups

This syrup is used in many Middle Eastern and Greek pastries. The orange flower water and rose water are traditional flavorings. Rose water can be very potent and should be measured carefully. Either flavoring may be decreased or omitted according to personal taste. This syrup is great on pancakes and waffles.

1 1/2 cups	water
3 cups	sugar
1 tsp	orange flower water*
1/2 tsp	rose water*
3 Tbsp	lemon juice
2 Tbsp	honey

Bring water to a boil in a medium pot. Add sugar and stir to dissolve. Bring to a boil again. Reduce heat to a simmer and add orange flower water, rose water, lemon juice and honey. Simmer for 1 minute. Remove from heat and set aside to cool. Syrup must be at least room temperature before pouring on filo pastries. If necessary, refrigerate the syrup for 20 to 30 minutes to cool it down.

*See Glossary of Ingredients page 166 & 167.

BIRD'S NEST BAKLAVA
Makes 25 to 30 Birds' Nests

3/4 cup	melted Clarified Butter (page 159), divided
2 cups	walnuts, chopped
1/4 tsp	cinnamon
1/8 tsp	nutmeg
1/8 tsp	cloves
2 Tbsp	sugar
1 lb	12x17" filo dough, defrosted (see Handling Filo Dough, page 161)
1 1/2 cups	Basic Syrup, cooled (page 137), divided
1 cup	raw pistachios, coarsely chopped

Preheat oven to 325 degrees. Brush a large, shallow baking pan with 2 Tbsp of the Clarified Butter.

Mix the walnuts with the spices and sugar. Set aside. Lay the filo dough on the table with the narrow side facing you. Starting at the bottom edge, grasp one sheet of filo with the fingers of both hands on top and your thumbs under the dough. Loosely gather the dough up to the top of the sheet. Hold one end of the gathered dough in your left hand and the other end in your right hand. Wrap the dough around three fingers of your left hand, tucking the end under the bottom of the Nest. Place it in the baking pan. Continue shaping the Bird's Nests until all of the dough is used. The size of the Bird's Nest will be determined by how tightly you roll the dough on your fingers.

Each Bird's Nest will take a heaping teaspoon of the walnut mixture. Place the tip of the teaspoon in the center of the Nest and push the nuts off, gently pressing them in place. Do not overfill, so there will be space to add the pistachios after Bird's Nests are baked. Drizzle a teaspoon of Clarified Butter around the edge of each Nest on the filo dough. Then drizzle any remaining butter over the tops of the Nests. Bake at 325 degrees for 25 to 35 minutes until golden brown. Remove from the oven and immediately pour 3/4 cup of the prepared syrup on the Nests. This should be done by slowly drizzling the syrup around the edge of each Nest on the filo dough. Place 1/2 Tbsp chopped pistachios on top of each Nest. Carefully drizzle the rest of the syrup over the top of the Nests.

CHOCOLATE BAKLAVA ROLLS
Makes 12 to 14 large rolls or 24 to 28 small rolls

1 15 oz jar	Nutella® Chocolate Hazelnut Spread, or other thick chocolate spread
1/2 cup	coarsely chopped pecans
1/2 tsp	cinnamon
1 lb	12x17" filo dough, defrosted (see Handling Filo Dough, page 161)
2/3 cup	melted Clarified Butter (page 159), divided
1 1/2 cups	Basic Syrup, cooled (page 137)
2 ounces	German Sweet Chocolate or other dipping chocolate
1/4 cup	finely chopped pecans

Preheat oven to 325 degrees. Brush a large, shallow baking pan with 2 Tbsp of the Clarified Butter.

Place Nutella in a bowl and mix in the pecans and cinnamon. If necessary, microwave for 30 to 40 seconds to warm it slightly for easier handling. Set aside.

For large Baklava Rolls, you will be working with full sheets of dough. For small rolls, place the unrolled stack of filo dough with the wide side facing you and cut the stack in half down the middle. To make rolls, remove two sheets of the filo dough and place on the table with the narrow side facing you. Brush the top sheet with Clarified Butter. Place 2 Tbsp chocolate filling (1 Tbsp for the small rolls) 1 inch up from the bottom edge of the dough. Fold the filo over on top of the filling. Then fold the side edges in. Brush the folded edges lightly with Clarified Butter. Roll to the end. Place the roll, seam side down, in the baking pan. Repeat brushing, filling and rolling procedure with the rest of the dough. The rolls will puff up when baked, so do not crowd them on the baking pan. When done making the rolls, brush the tops with additional Clarified Butter. Bake for 25 to 30 minutes until lightly browned.

Remove from oven and immediately drizzle with the prepared syrup. Microwave the German Sweet Chocolate on medium power for about 45 seconds or until melted. Drizzle the chocolate on top of the rolls. Sprinkle with the finely chopped pecans.

GALATOBOUREKO
(Greek Custard in Filo)
Makes 12 servings

3 cups	milk
1/2 cup	farina (cream of wheat)
1/2 cup	sugar
1/4 cup	butter
1 tsp	vanilla
1/2 to 1 tsp	lemon zest
6	eggs
2/3 cup	Clarified Butter, melted (page 159)
1 lb	12x17" filo dough, defrosted (see Handling Filo Dough, page 161)
1 1/2 cups	Basic Syrup, cooled (page 137)

Preheat oven to 350 degrees.

Place the milk, farina, sugar, butter, vanilla and lemon zest in a medium saucepan. Cook over medium heat, stirring constantly until mixture comes to a boil. Reduce heat and simmer for 1 to 2 minutes. Set aside to cool slightly.

Place eggs in a large saucepan and whisk until frothy. Gradually whisk in the milk and farina mixture. Set aside. The mixture will be fairly thin and will thicken when baked.

Brush a 9x12 inch baking pan lightly with Clarified Butter. Place two sheets of filo dough in the buttered pan with the filo extending up the sides of the pan. Brush generously with the Clarified Butter. Place two more sheets in the pan and brush with butter again. Repeat the layering and buttering until 12 sheets are used. Spread the custard filling evenly over the dough. Turn the edges of the dough in to enclose the custard.

Cut the rest of the filo to fit the pan. Lay the scraps on top of the custard and drizzle with butter. Next, lay 2 sheets of the cut filo on top of the custard and brush with butter. Repeat the layering and buttering procedure until all of the filo is used. Pour any leftover butter on top. Bake the Galatoboureko until golden brown, about 45 to 50 minutes. Remove from oven. Using a sharp knife, cut into 3 rows lengthwise and 4 rows widthwise. Slowly pour the prepared syrup over the top. Galatoboureko may be served warm or at room temperature. Leftover Galatoboureko should be covered tightly and refrigerated.

KANAFI
(Shredded Filo Dough with Cheese)
Makes 15 servings

This easy to prepare cheese dessert is called **KATAIFI** in Greek and is sometimes made with walnuts (the same filling as in baklava) instead of cheese. Either way, it is especially delicious served warm.

1 lb	kataifi dough,* defrosted
1 1/4 cups	Clarified Butter, melted (page 159)
1 1/2 lb	sweet white cheese* or mozzarella
1 lb	ricotta cheese
1/2 cup	coarsely chopped raw pistachios
2 cups	Basic Syrup (page 137)

Preheat oven to 350 degrees. Spray a 12x18 inch baking pan with non-stick spray.

Pour 1/4 cup Clarified Butter on the bottom of the baking pan. Cut the kataifi dough into 1 inch pieces and separate the strands. Distribute half of the dough on the bottom of the pan. Drizzle with 1/4 cup more Clarified Butter. Slice the sweet white cheese or mozzarella and arrange over the kataifi dough in the pan. Spread the ricotta over the sliced cheese. Distribute the rest of the dough on top of the cheese. Drizzle with the remaining Clarified Butter.

Bake for 20 to 25 minutes. Place under broiler for 2 to 3 minutes until the top begins to brown. Remove from oven and cut into 3 rows lengthwise and 5 rows widthwise. Pour 1 1/2 cups of the prepared syrup over top. Sprinkle with the chopped pistachios. Serve immediately. Pass the extra syrup in a bowl for those who prefer more.

Kanafi is best served hot out of the oven. Unbaked Kanafi may be stored, well wrapped, in the refrigerator for 1 to 2 days. Remove from refrigerator about 30 minutes before baking to bring to room temperature.

*See Glossary of Ingredients page 166 & 167.

KOULOURAKIA
(Greek Sesame Cookies)
Makes 40 to 45 cookies

4 1/2 to 5 cups	flour
1/2 tsp	salt
1 tsp	ground mahlab (mahlapi)* OR 1/2 tsp mistika,* crushed with 1 tsp sugar
2 1/2 tsp	baking powder
1 cup	butter, softened (2 sticks)
1 cup	sugar
3	eggs
2 tsp	vanilla

Glaze:

1	egg
2 Tbsp	water
1/2 cup	sesame seeds

Preheat oven to 350 degrees. Line 2 cookie sheets with parchment, or use foil and spray with non-stick spray.

Mix Dough: Place 4 1/2 cups of the flour in a bowl and mix in the salt, baking powder, and mahlab or mistika. Set aside. Place the butter and sugar in the bowl of an electric mixer. Beat on medium speed until light and fluffy. Add the vanilla and eggs, one at a time, beating well after each addition. Gradually stir in the flour mixture. Mix in more flour, as needed, to make a soft, pliable dough. If the dough seems too stiff as you are shaping it, knead in 1 or 2 Tbsp water.

Shape Cookies: Break off a piece of dough about the size of a walnut and roll into a 7 to 8 inch rope. Fold it in half and twist into a corkscrew shape. Place the cookie on the prepared baking pan. Repeat with the rest of the dough, placing the cookies 1/2 inch apart.

Glaze and Bake: Prepare the glaze by beating the egg and 2 Tbsp water in a small bowl. Brush the tops of the cookies with the beaten egg mixture. Sprinkle with sesame seeds. For more even baking, it is best to bake one tray at a time. Bake 25 to 30 minutes or until lightly browned. Transfer to a cooling rack. Store the cookies in an airtight container. They may be frozen for up to 2 months.

*See Glossary of Ingredients page 166.

PAXIMATHIA
(Greek Biscotti)
Makes 35 to 40 cookies

Paximathia are great for dunking in coffee or tea. The flavor can be varied by substituting anise or orange zest for the cinnamon and cloves.

1/2 cup	sugar
2 tsp	ground cinnamon
4 1/2 to 5 cups	flour
2 1/2 tsp	baking powder
1 tsp	ground cinnamon
1/2 tsp	ground cloves
1 cup	slivered almonds or coarsely chopped walnuts
1 cup	butter, softened (2 sticks)
1 cup	sugar
2 tsp	vanilla
3	eggs

Preheat oven to 350 degrees. Line 2 cookie sheets with parchment, or use foil and spray with non-stick spray.

Place the 1/2 cup sugar in a small bowl and mix in the 2 tsp cinnamon. Set aside.

Prepare Dough: Place 4 1/2 cups of the flour in a bowl and mix in the baking powder, spices and almonds or walnuts. Set aside. Place the butter, sugar and vanilla in the bowl of an electric mixer and beat on medium speed until light and fluffy. Add the eggs, one at a time, beating well after each addition. Gradually stir in the flour mixture. Mix in more flour as needed to make a soft, pliable dough.

Shape Logs and Bake: Divide the dough into three portions and shape each portion into a log about 14 inches long. Place 2 logs on one cookie sheet and one log on the other. Flatten to about 1/2 inch thick. Place cookie sheets in oven and bake for 25 minutes, rotating trays after 15 minutes. Remove trays from the oven and *allow to cool for 5 minutes.* Carefully transfer the loaves to a cutting board. Using a sharp searated knife, cut diagonally into 1/2 inch slices. Place the slices flat on the cookie sheets. Sprinkle with half of the cinnamon and sugar mixture. Bake for 8 minutes. Turn the cookies over and sprinkle again with the cinnamon and sugar. Return the trays to the oven and bake for another 8 minutes or until the cookies are dry. Transfer to a cooling rack and cool thoroughly before storing in a tightly covered container. They may be frozen for up to 2 months.

FINIKIA
(Greek Honey Cakes)
Makes 35 to 40 cookies

Also called **MELAMAKARONA**, these Greek Honey Cakes are always included on holiday dessert tables in Greece.

Dough:

5 cups	flour
3/4 tsp	salt
4 tsp	baking powder
1/2 tsp	baking soda
1 Tbsp	ground cinnamon
1 1/2 cups	vegetable oil
1 cup	sugar
1 cup	orange juice
2 Tbsp	cognac or bourbon

Nut Topping:

2 cups	finely chopped pecans
1/4 cup	sugar
1 tsp	ground cinnamon

Honey Syrup:

1 cup	water
2 Tbsp	lemon juice
2 cups	sugar
1 cup	honey

Preheat oven to 350 degrees. Line 2 cookie sheets with parchment, or use foil and spray with non-stick spray.

Mix Dough: Place the flour in a bowl and mix in the salt, baking powder, baking soda and cinnamon. Set aside. Place the oil, sugar, orange juice and cognac in the bowl of an electric mixer and mix on medium speed until well blended. Gradually stir the flour mixture into the oil and sugar. Add a little more flour, if needed, to make a soft, pliable dough.

Shape and Bake: Break off a piece of dough about the size of a large walnut and form into an oval shape. Flatten the cookie to about 1/4 inch. Place it on the cookie sheet. Repeat with the rest of the dough, placing the cookies about 1/2 inch apart. Bake for 25 to 30 minutes, until lightly browned. Remove from oven and let them cool on the cookie sheets.

Nut Topping and Honey Syrup: Place the Nut Topping ingredients in a small bowl and mix. Set aside. Place honey syrup ingredients in a medium saucepan and bring to a boil. Simmer 2 to 3 minutes. Leave syrup on very low heat and place 4 or 5 baked Finikia in the hot syrup for about 1 minute. Using a slotted spoon, lift them out, one at a time and press 2 tsp of the nut mixture on top. Set the cookies on a rack to drain. If softer, sweeter Finikia are desired, allow the cookies to soak a little longer. Store the Finikia in an airtight container. They may be frozen for up to 2 months.

KOURAMBIEDES
(Greek Wedding Cakes)
Makes 50 to 60 cookies

2 cups	Clarified Butter, melted (page 159)
4 cups	powdered sugar (1 lb)
2 Tbsp	cognac or bourbon
3 1/2 to 4 cups	flour
2 cups	slivered almonds, lightly toasted and chopped
1/4 cup	whole cloves (optional)
2 cups	powdered sugar for coating cookies

Place Clarified Butter in the bowl of an electric mixer. Cover with plastic wrap and chill until almost firm. While Clarified Butter is chilling, place almonds in a frying pan and toast over medium heat, stirring frequently, until golden brown. Remove from pan and set aside to cool thoroughly.

Mix Dough: When the butter is chilled, preheat oven to 325 degrees. Beat the butter on low speed briefly, then on high speed for 1 minute until fluffy and very light colored. Reduce the speed to low and stir in the cognac or bourbon. Gradually mix in 4 cups powdered sugar. Increase speed to high and beat for 1 minute until mixture is fluffy. Using a wooden spoon, stir in the flour and the toasted almonds. The dough should be pliable and not sticky. If necessary, mix in a little more flour so it will handle easily.

Shape and Bake: Shape the dough into walnut-size balls and place on an ungreased cookie sheet 1/2 inch apart. Press a whole clove in the top of each cookie, if desired. For more even baking, it is best to bake one tray at a time. Bake for 20 to 25 minutes until very lightly browned on the bottom. The tops of the cookies should be almost white. Remove from oven and allow to cool thoroughly on the cookie sheet. The cookies are very soft and buttery when warm, and cannot be handled until they are cold. It is a good idea to place the cooled tray in the refrigerator for about 5 minutes before handling. Kourambiedes absorb surrounding odors very easily, so don't leave them in the refrigerator too long. Roll the cookies in powdered sugar before serving.

Store the cookies in an airtight container. They may be frozen for up to 2 months.

MAMOUL
(Walnut-filled and Date-filled Cookies)
Makes 30 to 35 cookies

In the Middle East, Walnut-filled and Date-filled Mamoul are prepared for holidays and special occasions. Women often get together to make enough for each family. They make a day of baking and socializing.

2 cups	semolina*
1 cup	Clarified Butter, melted (page 159)

1 3/4 cups	flour
3/4 cup	powdered sugar
2 1/2 tsp	orange flower water*
1/2 cup	water

powdered sugar for dusting cookies

Place the semolina in the bowl of an electric mixer and mix in melted Clarified Butter. Cover and let it sit, unrefrigerated, overnight.

The next day, preheat the oven to 325 degrees. Add the flour, powdered sugar, orange flower water and water to the mixer bowl. Mix on medium speed for 2 to 3 minutes, until well blended. The dough should be fairly soft. Allow it to rest for 5 to 10 minutes, until it stiffens up. If the dough is still too soft to handle, mix in a little more flour. Pinch off a piece of dough the size of a golf ball. Press a large indentation in the center. Fill with 2 tsp walnut or date filling (below) and close up.

Shape the filled balls of dough according to one of the following methods.

Method One: Roll Walnut Mamoul into an oval shape and Date Mamoul into a round ball. Flatten the cookies to about 1/2 inch and place them 1/2 inch apart on an ungreased cookie sheet. Prick with a fork 4 or 5 times to decorate the top.

Method Two: Carved wooden molds, available at Middle Eastern groceries, are the traditional way to make Mamoul. Walnut Mamoul are made in a dome-shaped mold and Date Mamoul are made in a flat, round mold. This makes it easy to distinguish between the two. The cookies sometimes have a tendency to stick to the inside of the mold. To prevent this, place 1/2 cup flour in a small bowl. Lightly dip the ball of filled dough half way into the flour. Shake off the excess flour. Gently press the floured side of the ball into the mold. The dough should be level with the mold, so the bottom of the cookie will be flat. Turn the mold over and tap the end sharply on the edge of the table, catching the cookie in your hand as it drops out. Mold sizes vary, so the size of the ball may need to be adjusted to fit. Place the cookies 1/2 inch apart on an ungreased cookie sheet.

For more even baking, it is best to bake one tray at a time. Bake for 15 to 20 minutes, until Mamoul are lightly browned. Remove from the oven and transfer to a cooling rack. Store the cooled cookies in an airtight container. Before serving, dust cookies lightly with powdered sugar. They may be frozen for up to 2 months.

Walnut Filling for One Batch:

1 1/2 cups	walnuts, chopped
1 Tbsp	Clarified Butter (page 159)
1 tsp	ground cinnamon
1/4 tsp	ground nutmeg
1/4 tsp	ground cloves
2 Tbsp	sugar

Place ingredients in a bowl and mix to combine.

Date Filling for One Batch:

3/4 lb	pitted dates
1 tsp	ground cinnamon
1/4 tsp	ground nutmeg
1/4 tsp	ground cloves
1 Tbsp	Clarified Butter (page 159)

Chop or grind the dates and place in a bowl. If the dates are very dry, place them in the microwave and warm them slightly until softened. Using your hands, mix in the spices and Clarified Butter.

*See Glossary of Ingredients page 166 & 167.

BARAZIK
(Arabic Sesame Cookies)
Makes 25 to 30 cookies

These buttery rich sesame and pistachio-topped cookies are a popular after school treat and great for tea time.

1 cup	unsalted butter, softened
1 cup	unsifted powdered sugar

2 cups	flour

1 1/2 cup	sesame seeds
1/2 cup	raw pistachios, finely chopped
2	egg whites

Preheat oven to 375 degrees. Line 2 cookie sheets with parchment, or use foil and spray with non-stick spray.

Prepare Toppings: Place sesame seeds in a large, shallow frying pan and toast over medium heat until golden brown, stirring constantly. Transfer to a shallow dish and set aside. Place the pistachios in another dish and set aside. Beat the egg whites until frothy. Set aside.

Mix Dough: Place the butter in the bowl of an electric mixer and beat on medium-high speed for 1 minute until light and fluffy. Reduce speed to low and gradually stir in the powdered sugar. Increase speed to medium-high and beat for 1 minute until mixture is fluffy. Stir in the flour and mix until well blended. The dough should be pliable and not sticky. If necessary, mix in a little more flour.

Shape and Bake: Shape the dough into walnut size balls. Gently flatten each ball in the palm of your hand to about 2 1/2 inches in diameter. While holding the cookie in your hand, brush it well with the beaten egg white. Sprinkle with pistachios, then press the coated side of the cookie into the sesame seeds. Place the cookie on the cookie sheet with the coated side up. Repeat with the rest of the cookies. Then gently dab more egg white on the top of each cookie. The extra egg white gives the Barazik a nice glazed look. Bake for 12 to 15 minutes until lightly browned. Remove from the oven and transfer to a cooling rack. Store the cooled cookies in an airtight container. Barazik freeze well for up to 2 months.

GREIBE
(Arabic Butter Cookies)
Makes 60 cookies

These almost white cookies have a wonderful melt-in-your-mouth texture. When baking them, be sure to remove them from the oven before the tops get browned.

2 cups	Clarified Butter (page 159)
4 cups	powdered sugar (1 lb)
3 3/4 to 4 cups	all-purpose flour
2/3 cup	whole blanched almonds

Place Clarified Butter in the bowl of an electric mixer. Cover with plastic wrap and chill until almost firm. Beat butter on low speed briefly, then on high speed for 1 minute until fluffy and very light colored. Reduce speed to low and gradually stir in the powdered sugar. Increase speed to high and beat for 1 minute until mixture is fluffy. Using a wooden spoon, stir in 3 3/4 cups flour. The dough should be pliable and not sticky. If necessary, mix in up to 1/2 cup more flour. If it is still too sticky, chill the dough until firm enough to handle. When you begin to shape the cookies, if your hands are very warm, rub them with ice and dry thoroughly.

Shaping Method #1: Take a piece of dough the size of a walnut and roll it into a thick rope about 4 inches long. Lay the rope on an ungreased cookie sheet and turn the ends in opposite directions to form an "S" shape. Press an almond in the middle of each cookie. Place the cookies about 1/2 inch apart. This is the traditional shape for Greibe.

Shaping Method #2: Shape dough into walnut size balls. Place on ungreased cookie sheet about 1 inch apart. Flatten slightly and press an almond in the center

Baking Instructions: For more even baking, it is best to bake one tray at a time. Preheat oven to 325 degrees. Bake for 12 to 15 minutes, until cookies are very light brown on the bottom. They should still be almost white on top. If the cookies are allowed to bake too long, they will become crispy and will not have the desired melt-in-your-mouth texture. Remove from the oven and allow to cool thoroughly on the cookie sheet. The cookies are very soft and buttery when warm and cannot be handled until they are cold. It is a good idea to place the cooled tray in the refrigerator for about 5 minutes before removing cookies. Greibe absorb surrounding odors very easily, so don't leave them in the refrigerator too long.

Store the cookies in an airtight container. They may be frozen for up to 2 months.

LOUKOUMADES
(Little Donut Balls)
Makes 25 to 30 puffs

These sweet little donut balls are popular in Greece and the Middle East, where they are called **AWAMEE**. Whatever you call them, they are a favorite with kids and grownups alike.

2	eggs
1 tsp	vanilla

1 cup	plain yogurt
1/2 cup	water

2 cups	flour
1 1/2 tsp	baking powder
1 tsp	baking soda
1/4 tsp	salt

vegetable oil for frying

1 1/2 cups   Basic Syrup (page 137)

In a medium bowl, beat the eggs and vanilla lightly. Add the yogurt and water and beat until smooth. Add the flour, baking powder, soda and salt. Beat just until smooth.

Pour oil in a medium saucepan to a depth of at least 3 inches. Heat the oil to 360 degrees. Drop teaspoonfuls of batter into the hot oil, using a rubber spatula to push batter off spoon. Fry 3 to 5 minutes until golden brown on all sides, turning puffs with a slotted spoon. Drain on paper towels.

Dip the puffs into prepared syrup and set on a rack to drain. If desired, some of the Loukoumades can be rolled in a mixture of 1/4 cup sugar and 1 tsp cinnamon.

HARESI
(Yogurt and Semolina Cake)
Makes 9x13 inch cake

This simple to prepare cake is also called **NAMOURA** in Lebanon and **BASBOOSA** in Egypt. It is a favorite, economical dessert for large gatherings.

1 cup	flaked coconut
3 cups	semolina*
1 1/4 cups	sugar
1/2 cup	Clarified Butter, melted (page 159)
1 1/4 cups	plain yogurt
2/3 cup	water
2 tsp	baking soda
1 1/2 tsp	orange flower water*
1 1/2 cups	Basic Syrup (page 137)
1/2 cup	finely chopped pistachios

Preheat oven to 350 degrees.

Place the coconut in a frying pan and toast lightly over medium heat. Measure all ingredients, *except the syrup and pistachios*, into a large mixing bowl. Mix thoroughly. Pour into an ungreased 9x13 inch baking pan. Bake for 25 to 30 minutes, until lightly browned. Remove from the oven and cut into desired size pieces. Pour the syrup evenly over top. Sprinkle with the chopped pistachios.

*See Glossary of Ingredients page 166 & 167.

GREEK PUMPKIN CAKE
Makes 10 to 16 servings

This is a great cake for Halloween or Thanksgiving.

1 cup	raisins
1/2 cup	hot water
3 cups	flour
2 cups	sugar
2 tsp	baking powder
1 tsp	baking soda
1/2 tsp	salt
1/4 cup	unsweetened cocoa, sifted
1 tsp	ground cinnamon
1/8 tsp	ground ginger
1/8 tsp	ground nutmeg
1/8 tsp	ground cloves
1 1/2 cups	Clarified Butter, melted (page 159)
4	eggs, well beaten
1 16 oz can	pumpkin (2 cups)
1 cup	chopped walnuts
	Orange Glaze (page 153)
1 recipe	Whipped Cream (page 153)

Preheat oven to 350 degrees.

Generously spray a tube pan or bundt cake pan with non-stick spray.

Chop the raisins and soak in hot water for a few minutes. Drain and set aside. Place the dry ingredients in a large bowl and mix well. Make a well in the center and stir in the Clarified Butter, eggs and pumpkin. Mix until ingredients are blended. Do not over-mix. Fold in the drained raisins and the walnuts. Spread the batter in the prepared pan and bake for 60 to 70 minutes, or until a toothpick inserted in the center comes out clean. Allow to cool for about 1/2 hour. Invert onto a cake plate. Drizzle with Orange Glaze (below) and serve with whipped cream.

Orange Glaze:

1 1/2 cups	powdered sugar
2 Tbsp	frozen orange juice concentrate, melted
1/2 tsp	vanilla
2 to 3 drops	orange coloring

In a small bowl, blend all the ingredients until smooth. If the glaze is too thick, add water 1/2 tsp at a time until thin enough to drizzle. Serve with whipped cream.

WHIPPED CREAM
Makes 2 cups

This recipe for whipped cream is very stable because of the added gelatin. It can be made one day ahead. Use it for any recipe that calls for whipped cream.

1 tsp	unflavored gelatin
1 Tbsp	hot water
1/2 pint	whipping cream
3 Tbsp	powdered sugar
1 tsp	vanilla
1/2 tsp	almond extract

Place the gelatin in a small bowl and stir in the hot water. Set aside to soften. Place whipping cream in the bowl of an electric mixer. Beat on medium-high speed until soft peaks form. Stir in softened gelatin, powdered sugar, vanilla and almond extract. Continue beating until thick. Do not overbeat or the cream will separate into butter and whey. Refrigerate, covered, until ready to use.

RAVANI
(Greek Cognac Cake)
Makes 9x13 inch cake

2 cups	flour
1 1/2 cups	farina (cream of wheat)
1 Tbsp	baking powder
2 tsp	baking soda
1 cup	butter, softened (2 sticks)
2 cups	sugar
9	eggs
3/4 cup	yogurt
1/4 cup	Cognac or Gran Marnier
1 recipe	Cognac Syrup (page 155)
1 recipe	Whipped Cream (page 153)
1/2 cup	sliced almonds, lightly toasted

Preheat oven to 350 degrees. Spray a tube or bundt cake pan with non-stick spray.

Blend the flour, farina, baking powder and baking soda together in a bowl. Set aside. Place the butter in the bowl of an electric mixer. Using the whisk attachment, beat on high speed until fluffy. Reduce the speed to medium and gradually beat in the sugar. Add the eggs, one at a time, beating well after each addition. Blend in the yogurt and Cognac or Gran Marnier. Spoon the flour mixture into the batter, mixing continuously on low speed, until blended.

Pour the batter into the prepared pan and bake for 40 to 45 minutes until a toothpick inserted in the center of the cake comes out clean. Remove from the oven and poke cake in several places with a thin knife. Pour the Cognac Syrup over the cake. It will seem like a lot of syrup, but it will absorb into the cake. Allow to cool about 2 hours before serving. Top each piece with a dollop of whipped cream and sprinkle with the toasted sliced almonds.

COGNAC SYRUP
Makes 3 cups

2 cups	sugar
3/4 cup	water
1/3 cup	frozen orange juice concentrate
1 tsp	vanilla
	zest of one lemon
2 Tbsp	lemon juice
1/4 cup	Cognac or Gran Marnier

Place all the ingredients, *except the Cognac or Gran Marnier*, in a medium saucepan and bring to a boil. Reduce heat and simmer for one minute. Remove from heat and cool slightly. Stir in the Cognac or Gran Marnier.

SLICED CITRUS
WITH HONEY AND ROSEWATER
Serves 6

2	navel oranges
2	tangerines
1	grapefruit
1/2 cup	honey (preferably Greek honey)
1/2 tsp	*SPICE BAZAAR MIDDLE EASTERN BLEND*
1/2 to 1 tsp	rose water*
6 sprigs	fresh mint (optional)
6 Tbsp	pomegranate seeds (optional)

Peel the fruit with a sharp knife, removing the white pith. Cut into 1/4 inch slices and arrange on individual serving plates, alternating the oranges, tangerines and grapefruit.

Blend the honey, *MIDDLE EASTERN BLEND* and rose water. Add a few drops of water if the mixture is too thick to blend easily. Drizzle 2 to 3 tsp honey mixture over each serving of fruit. Garnish with mint sprig and sprinkle with pomegranate seeds.

*See Glossary of Ingredients page 167

MIXED FRUIT WITH YOGURT AND HONEY
Makes 8 to 10 cups

1 15 oz can	crushed pineapple in juice
1/2 cup	frozen orange juice concentrate, defrosted
1 cup	red seedless grapes
1 cup	strawberries
1	apple, cored
1	pear, cored
1	banana, peeled
1	orange, peeled
1	grapefruit, peeled
2 cups	plain yogurt
1/2 cup	honey (preferably Greek honey)
1/2 cup	chopped pistachios

Place the crushed pineapple with its juice in a large bowl. Stir in the orange juice concentrate. Add the strawberries and grapes. Cut the rest of the fruit into bite-size pieces and add to bowl. Gently mix the fruit and refrigerate, covered, until serving time.

When ready to serve, place 1 cup fruit in each bowl and top with 1/4 cup yogurt. Drizzle 1 Tbsp honey over yogurt and sprinkle with chopped pistachios.

FROUTAKE YOURTI
(Yogurt with Fresh Berries)
Makes 6 servings

2 cups	plain yogurt
6 Tbsp	honey (preferably Greek honey)
2 cups	blueberries, raspberries, blackberries or sliced strawberries

For each serving, place 1/3 cup yogurt on a dessert dish. Drizzle with 1 Tbsp honey. Top with 1/3 cup berries.

Include Froutake Yourti on your next buffet dessert table. Spread the yogurt on a platter, drizzle with honey and top with berries. It is a beautiful, refreshing alternative for those who prefer a light dessert.

TIPS, TRICKS
AND SPECIAL RECIPES

GLOSSARY AND INDEX

CLARIFIED BUTTER
(Ghee)

Clarified Butter does not need to be refrigerated. Store it in an airtight container in a cupboard or on your kitchen counter. It may be used in place of regular butter in any recipe in this book. One advantage to using Clarified Butter rather than plain salted or unsalted butter is that it doesn't burn when sautéing nuts and other ingredients. It should always be used in filo recipes because the water in salted or unsalted butter will cause the filo to become soggy. Pastries that specify Clarified Butter will not bake as well with plain butter.

To make 3 to 3 1/2 cups of Clarified Butter: Place 2 lb butter (or margarine if you prefer) in a large, deep microwave-safe bowl. The bowl should be large enough to allow the butter to foam up without overflowing. Microwave on medium power for 6 to 8 minutes until completely melted and hot. Remove from microwave and allow to sit for 10 minutes while the milk solids and liquids settle to the bottom. Skim off any foam that has formed on top, and discard. Carefully pour off or ladle out the clear butter. Discard the milk solids and liquids left at the bottom of the bowl.

BÉCHAMEL SAUCE
(White Sauce)
Makes 2 cups

Many dishes are enhanced with the addition of a good Béchamel Sauce, which is commonly known as "white sauce". The addition of SHAFIK'S *RED LENTIL SOUP SPICE* rounds out the flavor and gives it a satisfying richness. Try this sauce on any steamed vegetables. Or add small bits of chicken or meat and some vegetables to the sauce and serve it over rice or noodles. Experiment by adding other *BLENDS*, such as *ATHENIAN GARDEN SPICE* or *HELLENIC HERB BLEND* to the sauce for flavor variety. For 8 ounces of uncooked pasta you will need about 1 1/2 cups of sauce.

1/4 cup	butter
1/4 cup	flour
4 tsp	*SPICE BAZAAR SHAFIK'S RED LENTIL SOUP SPICE*
2 cups	milk

In a small saucepan, melt butter over medium heat. Add the flour and *SHAFIK'S RED LENTIL SOUP SPICE* and stir briskly until bubbly and smooth. Remove from heat and slowly add milk, whisking continuously. Return to heat, whisking continuously until mixture comes to a boil. Reduce heat and simmer until sauce is thickened.

ARABIC COFFEE
(Also known as Turkish Coffee)
Makes 4 cups

Coffee in the Middle East and Greece is served in small (demitasse) cups and is thick, dark and usually sweet. It is prepared in an **Ibrik***, a long-handled, tapered pot. The Greek style is a lighter roast and does not have the cardamom added.

4 Tbsp	Arabic or Turkish Coffee (finely ground coffee)*
4 tsp	sugar
1/8 tsp	ground cardamom

Measure 4 demitasse cups of water into an **Ibrik**. Add the sugar and cardamom and bring to a boil. Remove from heat and briskly stir in coffee. Bring to a boil, stirring gently. When the coffee starts to rise, remove the **Ibrik** from the heat immediately (do not let it boil over.) Give a quick stir, return to the heat and bring just to the boiling point again. Repeat a third time. Skim the foam off the top and place a little in each cup. Allow the coffee to rest for a minute. Then pour the coffee into the cups.

If you do not have an **Ibrik**, any small pot may be used, however the coffee may not foam up in the traditional way.

*See Glossary of Ingredients page 165.

HANDLING FILO DOUGH

Many people hesitate to work with filo dough because they have had difficulties with it in the past, or have heard others speak of problems they have experienced. By following these guidelines, you will soon become comfortable working with filo and your baking will go quickly and smoothly.

Purchasing Filo:
A Middle Eastern or Greek grocery store is the best place to buy filo. Specialty markets understand the care that is needed to store filo, and the chance of getting dough that sticks together is greatly reduced.

Storing Filo:
Filo may be stored in the freezer for up to 4 months or in a refrigerator for up to 1 month. If you plan to keep your filo in the freezer, place it there as soon as possible after purchasing. Do not place half-defrosted filo in the freezer. Refrigerate it until ready to use. Defrosting and refreezing filo creates condensation, which causes the dough to stick together. When ready to use filo, defrost it overnight in the refrigerator.

Handling Filo:
Since filo dries out quickly when exposed to air, be sure to have your work area clear and all of your ingredients prepared and ready to use before opening the package. Unroll the filo onto a dry cutting board. If any edges are stuck together, take a sharp knife and cut them away. Remove the number of sheets you will need immediately and cover the remaining sheets with waxed paper and then a very slightly damp towel. If you don't need the entire package of filo for your recipe, wrap the unused portion completely in plastic wrap and place it back in its box. Store in the refrigerator for future use. Do not refreeze.

Making Filo-wrapped Foods:
Clarified Butter should always be used in filo recipes. A good quality pastry brush should be used to brush Clarified Butter on the filo. Brushes are available in varying widths from kitchen and restaurant supply stores. When baking filo, the layers should bake evenly to a golden or medium brown color. Do not allow the filo to get too dark, or it will develop a bitter taste. Oven temperatures vary, so if the pastry is browning too quickly on top, reduce the temperature 15 to 25 degrees.

TIPS TO MAKE YOUR COOKING EASIER

1. Spices and blends should be kept in a cool, dry place. While many people keep their spices directly over their stove for convenience, it is not the best place. The heat generated from cooking will cause spices to deteriorate more quickly. Avoid shaking spices and blends directly over a steaming pot. The moisture will cause them to lump up. Shake the spice into your hand and then into the pot. Opened spices and blends are good for about 1 year. After that, the quality and flavor will deteriorate. Let your nose be your guide. If there is little or no aroma, you will probably get little or no flavor.

2. When marinating foods, place the food and the marinade in a gallon size zip-lock plastic bag. Close the bag and place it on a plate in the refrigerator. Whenever you open the refrigerator, turn the bag over and you will redistribute the marinade for a much tastier finished dish. An extra bonus is no bowl to wash at dinnertime.

3. Many recipes call for toasted pine nuts or other nuts. This is easily done on the stove in a frying pan. Toast on medium heat and stir frequently. Do not allow the nuts to become too dark or they will taste bitter. Remove the nuts from the frying pan as soon as they are toasted and place on a plate or tray to cool. Another method for toasting the nuts is to place them on a tray and brown them in a preheated 325 degree oven for 10 to 12 minutes. Shake the pan every 5 minutes for even browning. Transfer the nuts to a plate or another tray to cool. Store toasted nuts in an airtight container in your refrigerator or freezer.

4. Most of my soup recipes call for sautéing celery and onions in oil. For the best flavor, it is important to brown them well. Prepare enough for three or four batches of soup at once in a large frying pan. Then place the cooked celery and onions in plastic bags and freeze them. This reduces your preparation the next time you make soup.

5. For an easy, odor-free way to crush garlic, try this little trick. Put the garlic cloves in a baggie and lay the baggie on the counter. Using the flat side of a large butcher knife, sharply slap the garlic several times. Then turn the sharp edge of the knife up and tap the garlic with the blunt edge of the blade several times. Next, cut a corner off of the baggie and squeeze out the crushed garlic. No messy cleanup. No garlic press to scrape clean. No smelly hands.

6. For easier cleanup of baked dishes, I suggest lining the pan with parchment (available at the supermarket or in kitchen supply stores), or using foil and spraying with non-stick spray. When dinner is over, just throw the parchment or foil away and give the pan a quick wash. For

recipes that require deglazing the pan, do not use foil, but be sure to spray with non-stick spray. For food that will be placed under the broiler, do not use parchment.

7. Dark baking pans absorb more heat and will result in a dark bottom on the food you are baking. For more even baking, line dark pans with foil. This is especially important when baking cookies.

8. For faster, easier cooking of dried beans and peas, add 1 tsp baking soda and 1 Tbsp oil to the water. The baking soda shortens the cooking time and the oil will decrease the amount of foam that forms on top of the beans. When cooking pasta, adding oil to the pasta water also helps minimize the foaming.

9. For those who prefer pitted Calamata olives in salads or in cooking, try this simple way to pit the olives. Place one layer of olives on a sheet of plastic wrap. Fold the plastic wrap over to cover the olives. Using the flat side of a large butcher knife, sharply tap the olives. They will break open, making it easy to remove the pits.

10. Parsley is used in many recipes. It adds flavor and color, as well as many vitamins. For easy preparation of parsley, hold the whole bunch under cold running water with the stems up. Then, with the water still running, swish the parsley leaves in the sink until the parsley is clean. Place the bunch on a cutting board and cut off the stems just below the rubber band or tie. Discard the cut off stems and remove any remaining large stems. Roll the parsley in a dish towel or spin it in a salad spinner to remove excess moisture. If parsley is to be chopped, it should be dry or the chopped parsley will be mushy. To store parsley, place it in a plastic bag with a paper towel inside. Leave the bag open and refrigerate in your vegetable crisper. It will keep for several days.

SUBSTITUTIONS

In recipes using canned tomato sauce, crushed tomatoes or diced tomatoes, it is best to use the type listed. If you do substitute one type of canned tomato for another, it may be necessary to make adjustments in the seasoning and water quantity.

Where chicken broth is indicated, you may substitute chicken or vegetable bouillon cubes and water. Since these are usually fairly salty, you may wish to reduce the salt in the recipe.

Recipes that call for garlic cloves refer to medium cloves. The quantity of garlic may be adjusted to suit your taste.

Where lemon juice is indicated, freshly squeezed gives the best flavor. However, a good quality bottled juice may be used.

Nonfat or lowfat sour cream, mayonnaise and yogurt work well in place of the full fat varieties in *SPICE BAZAAR* recipes. The result may be a thinner sauce or dip.

Many recipes can be adapted suit vegetarian (◆) or vegan (✿) diets by substituting oil for butter, or using various soy-based meat substitutes. There are many excellent soy products available that could fool even an ardent meat-eater.

WEIGHTS AND MEASURES
(All measurements are level and standard)

3 teaspoons (tsp)	=	1 Tablespoon (Tbsp)
4 Tbsp	=	1/4 cup
5 1/3 Tbsp	=	1/3 cup
8 Tbsp	=	1/2 cup
16 Tbsp	=	1 cup
1 cup	=	1/2 pint
2 cups	=	1 pint
4 cups	=	1 quart
4 quarts	=	1 gallon
2 Tbsp	=	1 ounce (oz)
16 ounces	=	1 pint
32 ounces	=	1 quart

GLOSSARY OF INGREDIENTS

Most ingredients for *SPICE BAZAAR* recipes are readily available at your supermarket. Some of the special ingredients are listed below and are available at Middle Eastern, Greek or Indian grocery stores and in many gourmet and health food stores.

Aleppo Pepper (also called **Middle Eastern Pepper**) is a mildly hot and very flavorful chile pepper from Syria. If it is not available, you can substitute mild to hot chile.

Arabic Coffee is a finely pulverized dark coffee. If it is not available, you can try using a French roast coffee, but it must be ground to a powder.

Balsamic Vinegar is an aged vinegar produced in Italy. It has a sweet and fruity taste with a balance of acidity and fine aroma. It adds wonderful flavor to salad dressings.

Bulgur (burghul or bulghur) is made from whole wheat that has been parboiled, then dried and broken into four grain sizes. #1 is the smallest grain size and is used for preparing Kibbie. #2 is for Tabouli Salad. #3 and #4 are for pilafs. Bulgur gives a wonderful nutty flavor to dishes and is a welcome change of pace when served in place of rice. When purchasing bulgur be sure that you choose the appropriate grain size for your recipe.

Couscous is often thought of as a grain. However, it is a pasta that is made from moistened semolina. The word Couscous also is used to describe Moroccan stews.

Fava Beans are available canned or dried in gourmet or Middle Eastern grocery stores. Other beans of your choice may be substituted.

Greek Coffee is a light roast fine pulverized coffee. It is prepared like Arabic Coffee, but without the cardamom.

Greek Macaroni is a long hollow pasta which comes in different diameters. #1 and #2 are the largest and most common sizes. They are used to prepare the popular Greek dish, Pasticcio.

Holy Bread Stamp. This is used to imprint a seal on each loaf of the Holy Bread that is used in Orthodox Church services. It is about 5 inches in diameter and is made of wood or plastic, with a special design carved in it. Holy Bread Stamps are available at some Orthodox Churches and in some Middle Eastern grocery stores.

Hot Pepper Paste is made from hot red peppers. It adds lovely color and a distinctive flavor to stews, and is especially delicious in the Muhammara recipe on page 9.

Kataifi-Kanafi Dough is a shredded dough that is sometimes called Shredded Filo. It is used in pastries.

Mahlab (Mahlapi in Greek) is the dried seed of the wild black cherry. It is used in sweets and in breads.

Mint used in recipes in this book refers to Spearmint. Do not use peppermint as a substitute.

Mistika (Mastika in Greek, **Gum Mastic** in English) is a resin that gives a unique and interesting flavor to breads and desserts. It must be pulverized before using. To do this, place the mistika and a teaspoon of sugar in a mortar and pestle and crush it to a powder. Or place the mistika and sugar between 2 layers of plastic wrap and slap sharply several times with the flat side of a large knife blade.

Mixed Zatar: See **Zatar** (page 167).

Mizethra (Dry Ricotta) is a large, hard ball-shaped cheese imported from Greece or Italy. It is grated before using.

Nutella® Chocolate Hazelnut Spread is a very popular spread in Europe and in the Middle East. It is becoming more common to find it in Middle Eastern groceries and gourmet food stores. If it is not available, any good quality chocolate spread can be substituted.

Olive Oil. Extra Virgin gives the best flavor to uncooked foods and salads because of its full flavor. However, the olive oil congeals when salad dressings are refrigerated. To overcome this problem, use half extra virgin olive oil and half salad oil (canola, corn, soy or other vegetable oil) in dressing recipes. Regular olive oil is satisfactory for cooking or frying.

Orange Flower Water (Mazaher) is made by distilling water over orange blossoms. It adds a special flavor and fragrance to desserts and drinks.

Orzo (Rosamarina) is a rice-shaped pasta that is used as a side dish and in pasta salads. It adds flavor and color when it is browned in butter or oil and cooked with rice.

Pomegranate Syrup (Dibs Rumman)is a very sweet-tart, dark syrup. It is sometimes referred to as Pomegranate Concentrated Juice. Use it in Fattoush and other salads, and add it to stews and chicken dishes. Grenadine is not a substitute for Pomegranate Syrup.

Rose Water (**Maward**), like Orange Flower Water is prepared by distilling water over rose petals. It is used to flavor desserts and drinks. Rose Water gives a definite rose flavor and should be used with care, as too much can be overpowering.

Semolina (**Smeed**) is the ground endosperm of hard wheat. It is used in desserts and also is used in making pasta.

Sesame Tahini Paste (**Sesame Butter**) is made by grinding lightly toasted sesame seeds. It is similar in flavor and nutritional value to peanut butter but thinner in consistency. If you are shopping in a health or gourmet food store, be sure the sesame tahini has been made from toasted sesame seeds. The "natural" or "raw" sesame tahini paste has a much blander flavor. If the tahini has separated in the jar with oil on top and a thick hard paste on the bottom, warm it briefly in the microwave. Then stir thoroughly. Or place the entire contents of the container in a food processor or blender. Process or blend until smooth. Refrigerate tahini after mixing, and it will stay more uniform.

Sumac is the dried berry of the sumac bush. It has a tart flavor and is used in sauces and sprinkled on salads, chicken and meats. It is also a main ingredient in Mixed Zatar (see Zatar below). Both Sumac and Zatar have been written up lately in several major gourmet magazines and are becoming more familiar in this country.

Sweet White Cheese is a mild, lightly salted fresh (not aged) cheese. It is used in Kanafi and also popular as a breakfast or appetizer cheese.

Tamarind Paste is made from the pod of an Indian evergreen tree. It has a pleasant sour taste that is somewhat similar to Pomegranate Syrup, but less sweet. It is used in Indian stews and also to make a refreshing beverage with sugar added.

Turkish Coffee is prepared in the same way as Arabic Coffee but usually is a darker roast.

Whole Wheat or Wheat Berries (**Ammah**) is available both unshelled and shelled. The Unshelled Wheat takes several hours to cook and is used for preparing Memorial Wheat. The Shelled Wheat cooks much faster and is prepared with raisins, nuts, sugar and spices. It is served as a dessert, a breakfast cereal and to celebrate a baby's first tooth.

Zatar is the Arabic word for Thyme. **Mixed Zatar** is made up of pure zatar (thyme), sumac and toasted sesame seeds. This flavorful and aromatic herb blend is mixed with olive oil and baked on pita bread, is used in a marinade for chicken, and is served with olive oil for dipping with pita bread for breakfast.

INDEX BY SPICE BLEND

◆ Denotes Vegetarian

❖ Denotes Vegan/Lenten

INDEX BY RECIPE

INDEX OF VEGETARIAN AND VEGAN/LENTEN RECIPES

✤ Denotes Vegan/Lenten

SHARE THE EXCITEMENT
OF SPICE BAZAAR BLENDS!

Tear out this page and give it to a friend.

ORDERING INFORMATION

To order from our complete line of
SPICE BAZAAR BLENDS,
or for additional copies
of this **Cookbook**
and information about our
beautifully gift-boxed assortments:

**Call 1-800-30-SPICE
(1-800-307-7423)**

Or Order Online at www.spicebazaar.com

Email: paymon@spicebazaar.com

Dealer inquiries invited

SHARE THE EXCITEMENT OF SPICE BAZAAR BLENDS!

Tear out this page and give it to a friend.

ORDERING INFORMATION

To order from our complete line of
SPICE BAZAAR BLENDS,
or for additional copies
of this **Cookbook**
and information about our
beautifully gift-boxed assortments:

**Call 1-800-30-SPICE
(1-800-307-7423)**

Or Order Online at www.spicebazaar.com

Email: paymon@spicebazaar.com

Dealer inquiries invited